P9-AQM-038

Grover Brinkman's
SOUTHERN ILLINOIS

WEEKENDS, Inc.
Salem, Illinois 62881

FIRST EDITION

To
My Wife Leona
A fellow gypsy who enjoys the backtrails as much as I do.

CONTENTS

Part VI — Ghost Towns

Part VII — Buildings and Bridges

Part VIII — Links to the Past

Preface

Consider this an informal fireside chat about the many interesting and historic facets of Southern Illinois, an area coming into its own very strong. Long has the region had rather an indifferent metropolitan press. Now, almost overnight, the image has changed. Industrialists already refer to Southern Illinois as "The New Ruhr Valley." The big-city newsman is suddenly aware of its importance. The man who has traveled the many backroads and trails of Southern Illinois knows it as a charming land of rolling hills, long vistas, an unspoiled segment of the nation never faced with a ghetto or the threat of a megalopolis . . . Its people are not unlettered yet they have a nostalgic charm that is very good, clean and honest, depicting a "close to the land" viewpoint; they cling to decency and religion. Big roads and small traverse Southern Illinois, so none of its beauty is isolated; it is there for the eye of the beholder, green meadows, clear lakes, a profusion of woodsland blossoms. As more and more people "discover" Southern Illinois, their voices are unanimous: why didn't we learn about it sooner?

Grover Brinkman

Part I
Nature's Wonders

A Land Called Egypt

A writer in a popular magazine recently referred to southern Illinois as "Little Egypt." The word "little" could have been deleted; Little Egypt was a belly-dancer at the World's Columbian Exposition at Chicago. Southern Illinoisans are justly proud of the referral, Egypt. But never "Little Egypt."

That symbolical area of southern Illinois known as Egypt was used as early as 1843; it is looked upon with pride by native southern Illinoisans, never as a personal Appalachia.

The exact boundaries of Egypt will perhaps ever be in dispute. But most natives will settle for that part of the state lying south of the Baltimore and Ohio Railroad, which runs east from St. Louis to Vincennes.

Figuratively, Egypt would be the southernmost quarter of the state, that scenic historic area once called back country. The origin of the name, too, will always remain a puzzle. There are as many as four versions:

Egypt takes its name from the location of such old-world cities as Cairo, Memphis, Thebes, Palestine and Karnak.

The area bears a marked resemblance to the delta of the Nile.

The name originated in the folklore of the inhabitants, or possibly because at one time southern Illinois supplied corn to the rest of the state during a severe crop blight, playing good samaritan to much upstate Illinois.

A clash of dates discredits the first reason entirely. Cairo was not established until 1837; Thebes until 1844. Karnak also is far from a "very old" town. Allegation to the word, Egypt, appears as early as

1843, long before the influx of settlers at any of these places.

Another point: Alleged similiarity between southern Illinois and the delta of the Nile is totally absurd! The Nile's delta is at least 90 miles in length, 120 miles wide. The alluvial "tip" of southern Illinois called Egypt is far smaller. The balance of the southernmost third of the state is rugged, hilly, an outcropping of the Ozarks plateau, and bears no resemblance to any type of delta terrain.

One more point: No true southern Illinoisan will permit the allegation that the name originated from "the intellectual darkness" of the area, or the folklore of its people. Southern Illinois had institutions of learning well in advance of other state areas. John Mason Peck founded his Rock Spring Seminary near Belleville in 1827. Four years later it moved to the Alton community to become Shurtleff College. McKendree, aged Methodist institution of learning at Lebanon, was established in 1828. The first historical society in the state was at Vandalia. So "the intellectual darkness" used by some writers in describing southern Illinois has no bearing at all.

The late John W. Allen of Carbondale, southern Illinois' dean of historians, writing in the Chicago Schools Journal in 1955, cited earlier and more detailed testimony relative to Egypt. Allen's source was A. D. Duff, prominent lawyer and judge of southern Illinois, who contributed an article on the origin of Egypt to the **Shawneetown Gazette** in the 1860s. According to Duff, the very long and severe winter of the "deep snow," (1830-31) delayed the planting of crops. The following summer was cool, and a killing frost came early in September to northern and central Illinois. The corn crop upstate was a complete loss. The settlers needed corn for feed, seed, and table cornbread. They turned to the southern tip of the state, where the crop had matured. As a boy living on a main road in Bond county, Duff said that in the Spring of 1832 he saw many wagons coming south empty and going back loaded with corn. These people were prolific readers of the Bible, and were reminded of the sons of Jacob resorting to Egypt for grain.

The Biblical reference is to the famine that struck the Mediterranean world while the tribe of Jacob resided in Canaan. Hearing of their plight, Jacob's son, Joseph, who held a high place in Pharaoh's court, sent money and raiment and "ten asses laden with the good things of Egypt, and ten she-asses laden with corn and bread and meat," so Jacob could lead his people to Egypt and eat "the fat of the land." If you care to check, you'll find it all recorded in the Book of Genesis.

The baleful effects of the winter of 1830-31 in all but southern Illinois is a matter of historical record.

Today, Egypt's population is about two hundred thousand. There are no precise boundaries, but the image is strong in at least eleven of the state's southernmost counties. It's a very special place, both to natives and visitors. The landscape, away from the floodplains, is rolling, hilly, scenic.

Illinois' Egypt might have a few things in common with its overseas name-alike. The climate is about the same. Ancient man lived here. But that's about all.

Although southern Illinois' Egypt is in no way a part of Dixie, it has always leaned toward the friendly, relaxed ways of the deep South. Magnolias grow in the south and they also flourish in Cairo; cotton grows here as well as tobacco.

The area has a few budding industrial complexes, but outside of that, the rural way of life predominates. Visitors seem impressed, both as to life style and environment.

Sprawling Shawnee National Forest is a new environmental giant, maintaining the rough, natural terrain of the area. Wild turkeys abound there, and there are areas so remote that one needs a guide to find them. Thousands of Canadian geese and ducks winter at wildlife refuges scattered throughout the region. Huge Lake Carlyle on the north perimeter of the area, and Crab Orchard deep in its southern segment, are immense bodies of water catering to both sportsmen and industry, not to mention the wild life that seeks their shelter. Most of Egypt's parks abound in exploring possibilities. Giant City is its own mecca of surprises.

There is history in Egypt as well, at Shawneetown, Cave-in-Rock, Thebes. There are Cherokee graves here, as well, grim reminders of the Trail of Tears. George Rogers Clark trod this ground, and left his mark. Not all visitors to Egypt stop to explore. But if you do, carry a large notebook and a good camera.

Bald Knob Cross is a mecca in Egypt, now pointed out by various air routes. Murphysboro has its Apple Festival; Ridgway celebrates with popcorn; Cairo has its Magnolia Festival, and Bald Knob its Easter Sunrise service that draws people from the four points of the compass.

Egypt really is a sleeping giant, in the act of awakening: new, navigable rivers, huge lakes, the gasification of its greatest commodity, coal. Egypt might soon lose its name. Already economists are dubbing it the new Ruhr Valley.

The Awakening

Let's presume the time is April, when dogwood is blooming all through southern Illinois, locking the door on winter. High in the cloud-laced sky, Canadian honkers

Come April and southern Illinois' dogwood is
a thing of beauty, all through the hill country.

etch an almost perfect V as they wing toward a summer sanctuary; a ruffled hen sparrow starts an early invasion of a martin house to claim occupancy before the little purple birds arrive from their long migration.

The Shawnee hills are awakening; dry leaves cling fast in lifeless tenacity to the oak trees, at last flutter earthward in the brisk breezes of Spring. Grandfather sheds his wooly coat for a lighter sweater. There is a new light of anticipation in his rheumy eyes: he has survived another winter.

Autumn is a sweet, sad season in southern Illinois, when old people study the sunsets and shiver in the heightening wind, visioning their own frail bodies pitted against the rigors of the cold, dark days ahead.

But Spring is just the reverse. The gales that came strong and sharp in November, playing nudist with the trees, suddenly have the softness of a woman's touch. The dead grass is being engraved with patches of green. Even the velvet moss on the shady side of the forest trees has a new, more brilliant sheen. The night becomes a subtle thing, with earthy smells teasing the nostrils and yellow-frocked stars winking down with their message of an encompassing eternity.

This is the season of rebirth in the hills from the Wabash to the Mississippi. Nature puts on a gay new calico dress, and there is a fresh buoyance in the step of humans. It is a beautiful time, one of slow but sure awakening. It is also a time of renewal of one's faith. The winter has been hard. Merely being alive is a joy in the bright new colors of Spring.

It is also a time to clean house, not only the physical cleansing but a scrubbing of the mind. It is a time to discard and abolish the drivel of dark, somber days that narrow one's horizon. It is a time of change, a time to drain the anti-freeze from the car's radiator, the moroseness of winter from the mind.

The crisp blue air sparkles with diamonds, until the rising sun chases away the magic; wild roses, crucified by the hand of winter, show a tinge of budding green against the rotting wood of an old stake-and-rider fence. A white-tailed doe, frightened since birth, lifts her head from the edge of the pond to listen to a dog, braying in the distance.

There is a feeling of newness, of cleanliness, in the land. There is an insidious wine in the air that is intoxicating in its message: God has touched the earth with a magic wand and life is blossoming from soil still cold and dank with the frost of winter. Even nature arises from the grave.

It's Dogwood time!

And back in the Shawnee hills, an old grandmother, her face wrinkled with the years, retells the story of the dogwood, that bit of legend that never grows old:

At the time of Christ's betrayal, these hill folk persist, the dogwood tree attained the size of the present day hickory, ash and oak. So firm and strong was the wood that it was chosen as the timber to be used for the crucifixion cross.

To be used thusly, for such a terrible purpose, greatly distressed the dogwood. Jesus, nailed fast to its ironlike wood, sensed this and in his gentle pity for all sorrow, said to it:

"Because of your regret and pity for my suffering, I make you this promise: Never again shall the dogwood tree grow large enough to be used for a Cross. Henceforth, it shall be slender and shall be bent and twisted, and its blossoms shall be in the form of a Cross -- two long and two short petals.

"And in the center of the outer edge of each petal there will be nail prints. In the center of the flower, brown with rust and stained with blood, will be a crown of thorns -- so that all who see it will remember that it was upon a dogwood tree that I was crucified. And this tree shall not be mutilated nor destroyed, but cherished and protected as a reminder of my agony and death upon the Cross."

That, in substance, is the legend.

The legend still rampant in southern Illinois back-country goes a bit further in its symbolism. Near each dogwood tree, they say, one generally finds a redbud. The hill folk call it the Judas tree. For legend persists that Judas Iscariot, after betraying Christ went out and hanged himself from the limb of one of these trees.

The flower of the dogwood is white, while the blossoms of the Judas tree are a vivid scarlet!

Scoff at the legend if you must; but don't scoff at the beauty of the dogwood season in Southern Illinois.

Giant City

A visitor to Giant City State Park suddenly realizes there are many things at his or her fingertips: camping, exploration, hiking, climbing, to name just a few. This is a huge, sprawling geological wonderland near Makanda that captures the interest of young and old. Its beauty is rugged at any season of the year; it has a historic past that adds to its allure.

For instance, very few people today remember a guerilla band which called itself the Knights of the Golden Circle. However, the fact remains that in the crucial days of the Civil War, its members rode far and wide, trying to organize a Confederate Army in the midwest. The deep canyons of what is now Giant City State Park was their hideaway. At that time only rough trails led into this un-explored "bad land." So the group soon turned the area into a frontier fortress.

Lying slightly south in the latitude of Richmond, Virginia, the area had many southern sympathizers. The knights broke up into various groups of night riders, visiting various southern Illinois communities in search of recruits. It was common practice to ride into a town, distribute treasonable literature, terrorize the people, and ride out.

Lighting a cigar with a dollar bill was a favorite trick of the leader to show the people the utter contempt they held for the Lincoln government and its currency.

Presumably printing presses were set up in some of the hidden canyons of Giant City, to turn out their treasonable literature. Strangely, the group was never apprehended. Neither local law officers or Union troops ever penetrated their hideaway.

Even today, after the erosion of more than a century, some of the mottoes of the group are faintly visible, chiseled in the cliff walls that tower upward more than 40 feet.

High on the rock, some bodyguard of Jefferson Davis chiseled: "Albert S. Thompson, Freemont Bodyguard, Feb. 22, 1862, A.D."

What is now Giant City State Park is somewhat of a geological freak. It is one of the few spots in the state which the great Illinoisan glacial ice sheet did not touch. This grinding, gouging, smoothing geological giant altered much of the topography of the state to a level or rolling plain. However, the rocky upheaval that is Giant City State Park today seemingly escaped. The bedrock strata, unburied by glacial deposits, stands weathered, ancient and unscathed by time.

Perhaps this is one reason why people from every state come to Giant City to see the huge rock canyons which resemble Old World streets. It is typical western terrain transplanted to southern Illinois.

In this boxlike canyon deep inside Giant City
State Park, subversive Confederates set up
printing presses during the Civil War. Before
this time, buffalo killers used the canyon to
stampede the animals to their deaths.

Geologically, Giant City is composed of sandstone overlaying shale. Called the Makanda, this presumably was laid down in the Pennsylvania Period, to a depth of one hundred feet or more. Below this is the Drury shale, a soft mud-rock easily eroded.

In the deep recesses of these canyon-like "streets," even the birds are few and quiet, and sunlight seldom penetrates. It is easy to visualize the scene a century ago -- unshaven, uncouth, musket-bearing men living in subversive outlawry, waiting for the day to overthrow the Lincoln regime. The tide of war dissolved the organization, but strangely none of the key figures in the Knights of the Golden Circle were apprehended.

Before this, in the days of the Indians, some of the box canyons served as buffalo traps. Animals were driven into the enclosures and later captured. At other times, herds were driven over the brink, and the animals fell to their deaths.

Don't visit Giant City State Park on the run: there is too much to see!

Heron Pond

To visit a cypress swamp, one would naturally think of Florida, Mississippi or some other southern state, much of which is coastal lowlands. But southern Illinois has a cypress swamp that could be a "little brother" to Florida's giant Everglades except for one thing -- no alligators. The huge cypress trees are there, towering upward straight as bamboo, so are the moccasins and other marsh denizens, and much of the tropic vegetation.

Isolated, non-existent as far as the uninformed tourist is concerned, this hinterland is something dramatic for southern Illinoisans, now that roads and trails have been cut in, allowing visitation by old and young alike.

Called Heron Pond, this cypress swamp spreads over more than 1,100 acres of virgin woodsland along an untamed stream called the Cache River, near Vienna, in Johnson County. Through the untiring efforts of an Illinoisan named John Schwegman and other conservationists, the swamp has at last been put under the protection of the state, preserved for posterity. Heron Pond is an almost unbelievable sight in a state that boasts of corn, wheat and soybeans but never mentions anything even suggesting a swamp.

According to Mr. Schwegman, there is a reason for the cypress swamp at this particular spot in southern Illinois. It happens to be the southernmost point to which the ice sheet advanced during the Pleistocene Period, or great ice age. Because of this geologic history, the Heron Pond area is a meeting place or crossroads for many plants from different parts of the nation. Here one may find club mosses from the north intermingling with bald cypress and other plants of the coastal floodplain far to the south. Plants from the eastern Appalachian forests and the western prairies also meet in this land between the two great rivers, the Mississippi and the Ohio, making the area a botanical crossroads of the Midwest. Heron Pond got its name from the many blue herons that roost and nest here.

Since most of the natural areas in Illinois have long since been converted to agricultural and urban use, it is important to preserve what few original land types still exist, for scientific, educational and aesthetic reasons. These purposes were considered when the General Assembly created the Illinois Nature Preserves Commission in 1963.

Since then, under the leadership of its executive secretary, Mr. George Fell, Illinois has acquired such outstanding areas as Vole Bog, Lusk Creek Canyon,

Goose Lake Prairie and Beall Woods.

Until Heron Pond and its adjoining Wildcat Bluff area was purchased by Illinois as a nature preserve, much of this swamp area was owned by the same family which originally settled it in the 1820s, soon after Illinois became a state.

There was no logging here, and the forest is virgin, something rare in southern Illinois. Some of the cypress trees tower upward for a hundred feet or more. People can view the swamp in complete safety, keeping to a board walk that leads out into the brackish water.

Besides the moccasins and other water snakes, the swamp contains beaver, river otter and bobcats, not to mention the giant herons. The cypress knees and fallen trees turned into mossy logs, depict great age and complete isolation from civilization.

For some unexplained reason, this area was spared from the northern glaciers, and offers steep hills of sandstone, caves and sinkholes. Filmy fern and small flowered rock pink are found only here, nowhere else in southern Illinois.

One is amazed at this terrain the moment he or she leaves their car at the parking site. The mile-long trail along the Cache River is an experiment in walking through virgin forest, with strange plants, birds of every description, and the quietness of a great woodsland undisturbed by man.

This watery wilderness in Johnson County, six miles southwest of Vienna, is a botanical wonderland for everyone who likes nature, and the men who were instrumental in preserving it should be praised.

If you visit Heron Pond, follow Illinois highway 45 south from Vienna to the Belknap Road. Turn right here, and watch for signs. A single-lane all-year road leads to a parking and campsite on a ridge. From here, one walks. The distance is about a mile, over a well-marked trail. Bring your own food and drink if you intend to spend the day here; wear good walking shoes. If one loves nature, you won't regret the visit.

Land's End

Usually a human being is awed by the majesty of nature: one feels the impact of a great, thundering waterfall, a deep, mysterious canyon, a snow-crested mountain. The joining of two great rivers induces the same aesthetic feeling, and when one stands at the water's edge at Birds' Point, the extreme southern tip of Illinois, and sees the waters of the Mississippi and Ohio mix in a wide cauldron of motion, the amazement is there. Much of the water of the entire nation meets at this strategic point.

There was a time when the Ohio and Mississippi here swarmed with steamboats, paddle-wheelers, with as many as a hundred riverboats docking at Cairo in a single day. This was indeed a romantic era.

Ten miles above Cairo was the Marine Ways at Mound City, where steamboats were built and kept in repair. The time began in 1859. When the Civil War broke out, the ways were taken over by the government. From commercial steamers the work turned to building gunboats. Iron smelted in the nearby Illinois Furnace was used in the armor.

Cairo took its name from Egypt, along with Karnak, Thebes and Goshen. Fort Defiance was born here, a Union stronghold that played an important part in the war between the states.

Today, Birds' Point is a pleasant recreation park, where one may see the great bridges spanning the streams at close hand, marvel at the gray waters of the Ohio pouring into the yellow flood that is the

Mississippi. This is the southernmost tip of Illinois, a narrow peninsula in Alexander County with an altitude of only 315 feet. Somewhat exotic for southern Illinois are Cairo's ginkgo and magnolia trees, its nearby canebrakes and cotton fields. Many visitors open wide their eyes when they learn that Cairo geographically is farther south than Richmond, Virginia or Tunis, Africa.

The city of Cairo itself is encircled by a huge levee that rises from the river delta like the ramparts of a walled town. Steamboats have whistled for a landing here since the 1840s, but now they are gone and huge dieselized tows take their place as the new commerce on the rivers.

Magnolia Manor, with its spacious old house, and the many ginkgo trees in Cairo are a wonder and delight to visitors. Here is a bit of tropical grandeur in southern Illinois.

Cairo has had its racial disputes, its unrest. But there is a graciousness about Cairo as well, a river town steeped deep in history and nostalgia. It knew the drama of the Civil War, and it has long felt the fury of two great rivers, sometimes placid, sometimes furious. The two rivers have laid an indelible image on Cairo; it is unlike any other town in southern Illinois.

Part II
Strange But True

Tower Rock

As long as the majestic Mississippi flows to the Gulf, the history of Tower Rock will fire the imagination of Illinoisans. Because of the treacherous currents surrounding it, "the rock" was feared by native Indians long before the first French missionaries and explorers beheld its beauty. Men have died here, boats have foundered. Each year the legends of Tower Rock grow.

And now at long last it seems that this island in the Mississippi channel, just off Grand Tower, Illinois, will be preserved for posterity. Several times in its long history man has sought to destroy it.

Because the famous rock, really a precipitous island, is surrounded by very treacherous river currents and whirlpools, only the most adventurous have scaled its rocky sides. One can see the rock from Grand Tower, but the only way to climb it would be to hire a boatman and take the chances involved. From the Missouri side, a one-lane farm road leads close to it, but it is far from a good one, and people with low-slung cars hesitate to use it.

But if you insist on seeing Tower Rock at close hand, a ferry at Grand Tower will take you across the river, to within camera range. Once the Jesuits had a tall cross here. Now, unless present plans go astray, another cross, to be illuminated at night, will adorn the crest, making the island visible far up and down the river.

The history of Tower Rock goes back to December 12, 1698, when three missionaries, De Montigny, Davion and St. Cosme, established a landing atop the rocky island. Since prehistoric times, the perils of the whirlpools at the rock have been notorious. The howling of the winter winds between the high bluffs was a never-to-be forgotten sound to the early river explorers.

Back in 1871, President Ulysses S. Grant issued an executive order to preserve the rock, thinking that some day it might be used for the piers of a bridge to span the river. The bridge never was built, but the executive order gave the rock the status of a national park. Thereafter, newsmen and other writers often referred to the rock as "The smallest national park in the nation," an honor that is not today recognized by the national park service.

At normal river stages, Tower Rock juts upward for about 65 feet. Its brushy top is less than an acre. As early as 1819, John James Audubon, naturalist-artist, wrote about Tower Rock and the treacherous river currents that swirled around it. Mark Twain, famed writer and river boat pilot who often stopped near Tower Rock to refuel his boat, often referred to it as "being spawned by the devil himself."

Across from Grand Tower, facing the famous rock, the Mississippi has thrown up a long, clean sandbar that is ideal for picnics and outings. Here, too, is a rocky cliff known as the Devil's Bake Oven. Also within sight is a gigantic twin pipeline bridge spanning the river that carries a major gas artery from Texas to Illinois. The town of Grand Tower itself is one of the few river towns in the state that projects its true image.

At long last, Tower Rock has been entered into the "National Register of Historic Places," and its development and preservation seems assured.

Tower Rock, once called "Smallest National
Park in the U.S.," as it looks today. The camera
faces the Illinois shore of the Mississippi.

Dr. Uriah Hurd had this odd stone placed on his grave at Sandoval, thinking it was a meteorite. The legend has since been disqualified by NASA. But the curious still come to visit his grave.

A Doctor's Unusual Tombstone

Tourists and genealogists, young and old, have a penchant to roam old cemeteries, hunting for old grave markers and tracing family trees. In the old section of the Sandoval Cemetery, just off of Route 51, tourists have long made a path to the grave of Dr. Uriah Hurd.

The reason? Dr. Hurd's grave, presumably, was marked with a huge meteorite that he dug up on his farm, sometime between 1858 and 1866. The huge boulder is mounted on a concrete base. One side has a small area polished smooth and the name "Hurd" engraved in large letters. On the other side of the stone, two round areas have been polished and the birth and death statistics of Hurd and his wife engraved.

The stone, presumably, was a meteorite. For more than half a century its legend grew in the Sandoval area. People from near and far came to view the odd monument. The sexton of the cemetery retold the story, as it was told to him, and most tourists snapped a picture or two of the unusual marker and went home to give the story wider publicity by telling it to his or her friends.

It might be called a mean trick for a reporter to research the story to the place where the legend fell apart, but such is the case.

Recently word of the unusual tombstone reached Elbert A. King Jr. of the geology and geochemistry section of the NASA Manned Spacecraft Center at Houston, Texas. He wrote the family requesting a fragment of the stone for analysis. After tests in NASA laboratories, he wrote:

"Our examination of the 'meteorite' indicates that it is a weathered diabase, an igneous rock, not of meteorite origin. It probably is a large glacial erratic. We are most interested in examining meteorites or suspected meteorites. We will happily examine small chips of any suspected meteorites free of charge, because meteorites are extraterrestial. Some must come from the moon and the asteriod belt and will doubtless be encountered in manned lunar or space exploration, hence our extreme interest."

A surviving relative of Dr. Hurd said that the doctor had firmly believed the stone to be a meteorite because when he found the stone it was partially buried and he had not noticed it before.

In shape and hardness it well could be a meteorite, but NASA says it is not. Thus a legend is defrocked in the interest of science.

But the unusual tombstone will still be visited by tourists in the coming years, for legends die very slowly.

A Wayside Shrine

A secondary road leading from Germantown north to its neighboring community of Breese suddenly is a mecca for tourists in southern Illinois. The reason is a bit unusual, simply a cross mounted by the side of the road, in a farmer's pasture.

But recently the cross has been updated. It is now a permanent landmark, made of concrete. A neat white fence encloses it, keeping out the cattle ranging in an adjacent pasture.

Local people, familiar with the cross, rarely stop. But tourists do. It's a large cross, about 14 feet high. Out come the cameras. Sometimes the inquisitive go up the lane to the farm house for more information.

It all started back in the cholera epidemic years that plagued the area, starting in 1832. People died in vast numbers, both in the cities and the rural areas. St. Louis, then a struggling waterfront town, had a death toll that reached as high as 601 in a single week. Entire families were wiped out in various southern Illinois areas. In some towns, death came so fast that burial teams were recruited to take care of the dead.

Week after week, the epidemic raced over the land. Streets were sprayed with lime, fires of tar and sulphur were kept burning; people used chloride of lime, vinegar and even coffee as a preventive, none of which had any effect on the disease.

It was during this crucial time that a very religious farmer who lived north of Germantown, Joseph Altepeter by name, made a covenant with his Maker. His large family had thus far escaped the disease. He prayed that if they were spared he would make a perpetual memorial to God as an evidence of his faith.

Miraculous or not, the Altepeter family was spared, although neighbors on all sides of them succumbed to the disease. Joseph Altepeter went out to a woods lot, cut down a tree and made a cross. With the help of his older children the cross was dragged to a spot near the public road and mounted, so all who passed could see the evidence of his faith.

That's been well over a century ago. Dozens of wooden crosses on the same spot have rotted away, always to be replaced. For Joseph Altepeter had a codicil in his will stating that whoever followed him on this prairie farm would maintain the cross. Down through the years, the request has been honored.

Now the cross is made of concrete, and promises to be there for a long, long time, mute testimony of one man's great faith.

Airborne Prophets

The towns of Waterloo and St. Joe, both in Monroe County, have large copper roosters atop two of their church steeples.

The stranger suddenly has a question. Why?

It might be mentioned that the two airborne roosters have nothing to do with existing airports in the area, or the probable building of new facilities. They've been up there long before the first airplane was invented.

It's not uncommon to see a southern Illinois church steeple topped with a cross, a weathervane or other religious symbol. Pinckneyville has a church steeple topped with an open Bible; Okawville has one with a trumpeting angel, Gabriel. But crowing roosters?

It seems that roosters were first used on European Protestant churches during the reformation as a protest. Purpose of the emblem was to remind those who saw it that it was Peter who denied Christ on the eve of The Crucifixion, when these denials were marked by the crowing of the barnyard cock.

By seeing the symbol, the observer would be reminded that any denial of Christ would be observed and marked. There may have been some remote connection between the belief held from pagan times that the rooster was highly prophetic.

In certain areas of Germany, roosters are fairly common on church spires, even today. But the idea was not generally accepted in the Untied States when suggested by immigrants from the "old country." Waterloo and St. Joe are two of the few spots in southern Illinois where the barnyard fowl "points the wind" atop a high church spire.

Neither the ice of winter or the near-tornadoes of summer has toppled this four-foot-high
rooster off this church spire at Waterloo. He's
been up there, pointing the wind, since 1874.

Waterloo residents say that the rooster was the work of a skilled German coppersmith named Louis Wall, who also is credited with making many of the large copper kettles still used in the community at apple butter cooking time.

The four-foot-high rooster at Waterloo went on its 125-foot-above-ground perch on St. Paul's steeple in 1874. Despite several near-tornadoes and many windstorms, the old bird still rides high above the town, easily visible to travelers on Illinois highway 3, which passes the church.

All through the years, its copper exterior has gathered a patina that delights all who admire the look of old and weathered copper. Some say that years ago, a swarm of bees got inside the rooster and used it for a hive. Steeplejacks who have checked the belfry say there are a few rifle holes through the big rooster, but it'll take more than a lead pellet to topple him from his perch.

South of Waterloo, off the highway, at the small crossroads community of St. Joe, located near the crossing of the famous Bellefontaine-Kaskaskia Trace, another large copper rooster graces the spire of Zion church there, presumably the work of the same coppersmith.

Some persons have lived at Waterloo for years, and are totally unaware that the barnyard fowl is up there, pointing the wind.

"What rooster?" a woman asked. "I've lived here 22 years; I haven't seen any rooster!"

The traveler, the historian, will be more observative. Seeing a large copper rooster atop a church steeple today is just about as rare as finding a gold coin in one's change; southern Illinoisans are justly proud of those two birds!

The River With Two Names

Ofttimes a single place-name can reveal the area's historic past. In this instance it reveals a rich French lineage.

With the canalization of southern Illinois' very crooked, very erratic "river of the big cat fish" nearing completion, the question arises: "Why was it first called The Okaw on its lower stretches, and then changed to The Kaskaskia?

Even today, the word "Okaw" still is visible on some of the ancient railroad bridges spanning the stream. The bridge shown here, at Roots, soon to come down, has the word painted on one of its steel girders.

But the Corps of Engineers, U. S. Army, the planners of the new river, never refer to it as The Okaw but always as The Kaskaskia. This is correct, for the latter name has been firmly established geographically, and will thus remain. Even so, there is a romance about its initial name, The Okaw, that is intriguing.

Perhaps the matter is explained quite well in an editorial published in the **Mascoutah Herald,** issue of September 8, 1897. The author is the late Hon. J. Nick Perrin, noted southern Illinois historian, who says:

"In the early days when Illinois was a part of the Indiana Territory, representatives were chosen who attended sessions of the Territorial Legislature at Vincennes. The then-inhabited portion of southern Illinois was mainly composed of the early French villages, ancient Kaskaskia being one of them.

"A trail through our state to the Territorial Capital was known as the Vincennes Trace. Legislators and travelers rode along this path on horseback, the only

This bridge, which carries the Missouri-Illinois railroad across the river at Roots, is plainly marked, OKAW. But the river is the Kaskaskia. By the time this sees print this bridge will be gone, to be replaced by a higher structure, so barging can start on the new, canalized river.

means of travel in those days unless one went on foot or in crude carts. The customary salutation and response along this trace finally gave rise to a new word, Okaw."

Why Okaw?

Kaskaskia (or Cascasquia as it was then spelled), was abbreviated into Cas, pronounced Kah. This was not only true in daily parlance but in many of the old Illinois territorial records, all dated at Cas.

Hence, when the French travelers along the new Vincennes Trace would meet, to inquire as to each other's destination, those going to the old French village would reply, "An Cas," (to Kaskaskia). "An" was pronounced "O" and meant "to," while "Cas" being pronounced "Kah," was the abbreviation of Cascasquia.

The response to "An Cas," of "O Kaw," was taken up by English speaking settlers and broadened. The linguistic change finally became the word, Okaw, which has clung to the lower river for well over a century.

But the change is final at last. Despite the romantic overtones of the word, it is already in discard, geographically. The river is the Kaskaskia, growing more famous each day, its wide basin already dubbed "the new Ruhr Valley," as the new boom era of coal-gasification and steel moves into southern Illinois.

Oldest Bell in the Nation

Restoration of the Old Chapel at McKendree College, Methodist institution of learning at Lebanon, gave a new home to what is presumably the oldest chapel bell in the U. S. Presumably, the bell was cast in Spain in the eighth century. Some historians accept this, others do not. Facts

here mingle with legends, but whatever is your reaction to the statement, one thing is indisputable -- it is an ancient bell!

The bell was taken out of the chapel belfry back in 1957 when a storm damaged the building. It was put on tour and upon completion of the trek was set up in the library building at McKendree until the chapel could be restored.

In this 118th year of McKendree College, the ancient bell has again been brought into sharp focus. The college points out that the claims of five different bells in the nation, all classed as "ancient," point out that the McKendree Bell is the sage of them all.

The other four contenders in age are the Florida Cathedral church bell in St. Augustine; the Maria Josefa bell in Santa Fe's San Miguel Mission Church; the bell at Fox Fields Estate near Philadelphia, and the St. Stephen Episcopal church bell in East Haddam, Conn.

By virtue of its date of casting and entrance into this country, the McKendree bell without doubt is the patriarch of all American bells, college officials claim.

Presumably the bell was cast in Spain in the eighth century, recast in the fourteenth, and brought to Florida two centuries later.

There is a lapse in history here. The bell disappeared, only to be discovered in a deserted mission in what is now the state of New Mexico by traders out of Santa Fe. Presumably the traders were east-bound, for they took the bell with them to St. Louis and sold it. Because it was damaged, it was recast by a man named David Caughlan.

Next mention of the bell is when it appeared on exhibition at the Illinois State Fair, then held in Centralia instead of Springfield. The date was 1858. Dr. N. E. Cobleigh, president of the then-young McKendree College, with one of his professors, purchased the bell for the college.

The bell called McKendree's students to classes for over a century. Then a windstorm wrecked the aging chapel and the bell was taken down from the belfry.

Now, mounted in a new bell tower, the bell is starting a second century of service at Lebanon.

In appearance the bell is 31 1/2 inches in diameter, 25 inches high, with a yoke of 16 inches. Strangely, the yoke is cast from the same type of metal used in the bell. There is a crown on top for hanging. One side reads: Saint Louis, Mo., and the other, David Caughlan.

The bell's actual history is clouded by gaps in its early environment, a fact that no doubt will remain unchanged in the future. For if there are any records as to the bell's early life they are lost in antiquity. But the fact remains it is the patriarch of bells and well deserves the esteem of a restored chapel to house its ancient metal.

Here is a chapel bell whose antiquity outshines all contenders. No wonder that visitors from far and near trod the campus of McKendree to see its ancient heirloom.

Saga of the Late "Mom" Hale

Charles Kuralt, America's roving TV reporter has proven that some of the most fascinating stories are often found buried in some crossroads community in rural America. Kuralt's itinerary so far has detoured the small southern Illinois river town where the late Melissa (Mom) Hale lived, but it's a story well worth any reporter's time and effort.

Mom Hale, residing at Grand Tower, a river community of less than a thousand people, until her recent death had served more than one and one-half million meals in her rural restaurant there. She is gone, but the restaurant goes on.

That isn't all. A monument recently erected in the front yard of her small

eatery, affirms the fact.

An adage hoary with age persists that if a man or woman builds a better mousetrap the public eventually will beat a path to his or her door to purchase it. This is easily proven in the case of Mom Hale.

Erected and unveiled in the yard of her restaurant-home in Grand Tower before her death is a testimonial plaque where the text says Mrs. Hale has served more than one and one-half million meals to the public since she first opened the eatery in 1940.

At the time, Mrs. Hale, 79, wasn't too excited about the monument near her front door, other than to say several old friends were responsible for it.

Wayman Presley, retired rural mail carrier of nearby Makanda, headed a group to bring a five ton boulder to the restaurant, where it was mounted in the yard and a bronze plaque attached to it, so all who came could read the message.

The full text on the marker reads: "Mrs. Melissa (Mom) Hale, who, for more than thirty years from 1940 served over a million and a half home-cooked all-you-can-eat meals to all comers on this site. Those of us who have enjoyed her cooking affectionately dedicate this plaque to her."

The restaurant now is operated by a son, Thomas Hale. Each week-end it serves a thousand or more meals to people who drive great distances to enjoy the family-style, all-you-can-eat cooking.

"I think it's awfully nice for so many people to be so kind to me," Mrs. Hale said, when the marker was placed. Then she added, wryly: "But whoever heard of a monument to a country cook?"

For years Mom Hale did all of the cooking, using the culinary arts she learned from her own mother, who was of German descent.

Mrs. Hale and her late husband came to Grand Tower in 1925 in answer to a news-

MRS. MELISSA (MOM) HALE
WHO, FOR MORE THAN 30 YEARS FROM 1940
SERVED MORE THAN A MILLION AND A HALF
ALL-YOU-COULD-EAT, HOME-COOKED MEALS TO
ALL-COMERS ON THIS SITE.

THOSE OF US WHO ENJOYED HER COOKING
AFFECTIONATELY DEDICATE THIS PLAQUE TO HER.

This plaque, mounted on a 5-ton boulder, was erected in the yard near the restaurant of Mrs. Melissa (Mom) Hale at Grand Tower, shortly before her death. It is in recognition to her long career, serving one and one-half million meals to the public. Tourists visiting southern Illinois rarely pass up the restaurant at mealtime.

paper ad asking for a responsible couple to supervise a dairy farm. She drifted into the restaurant business in a small way, with three tables in a room of the family home. The business grew -- and grew.

Today, people drive great distances to eat at Mom Hale's restaurant. They stand patiently in line in the shaded yard, waiting to get inside.

There is nothing fancy, merely good home-cooked food in copious quantity. A sign on the entrance door says "No Liquor!" and means it.

One goes in, finds a table. A waitress asks your choice of meat. You make a choice and wait. And soon the food comes in, everything from home-grown vegetables in season to hot biscuits and jam. Pie is part of the meal, not an extra. When you've eaten your fill you pay a very nominal charge, and decide you must come back at the first opportunity.

Grand Tower is a quaint, charming river town with a long, historic past, both turgid and mellow. It was once an iron smelting town, but no more do its once-busy furnaces belch smoke. Down on the levee, the Devil's Backbone pokes rocky fingers at the swirling river. Grand Tower itself sits behind the levee, protected from the river. Mark Twain often visited here as a riverboat captain; John James Audubon painted eagles in the crags here long before the town was born; a power plant north of the town, and a huge skyline bridge across the river here add a new economic image. The bridge, incidentally, is not a highway structure. Instead its high web-laced towers carry twin gas lines of a pipeline facility across the river from Missouri into Illinois. One could see the river from Mom Hale's restaurant if it wasn't for the levee. If you climb the levee and linger there you'll see the extensive barge traffic on the river, barges enroute to New Orleans or northward to St. Louis.

Eating at Mom Hale's in Grand Tower is an unforgettable experience, and one you'll remember for a long time.

A million-and-a-half meals is a lot of food!

A Three Dollar Bill

As phony as a three dollar bill?

You've heard the expression many times. This writer admits to being guilty of using this old cliche as well, dramatizing some bit of action in a story.

This is his solemn promise that it will never happen again!

There was a three dollar bill! A very legitimate one, too!

This odd-denomination currency was issued in southern Illinois, at the first territorial bank at Old Shawneetown. Some of the ancient bills are still in existence, as well. The rotting building inside of which they were issued is a crumbling ruin near the Ohio River levee at Shawneetown, awaiting restoration as a historic landmark.

There also was a four dollar bill, a six, seven, eight and nine dollar bill, unbelievable as it sounds today!

Even our recently-withdrawn two dollar bill is a collector's item, but how would you like to paw through a billfold containing the above mentioned odd-currency in paying a bill at the supermarket or garage?

The forefathers of our present currency system evidently had a far different viewpoint relative to this old-time paper money.

Whenever the question of finances rises in any discussion today, someone always is ready to point out that we have a constantly shrinking dollar, which is true, presenting a problem to the man who brings home his paycheck each fortnight. But this problem recedes quickly when

Howard Mayes, a curator at the Docker Museum, showing a sheaf of odd-denomination bills issued by the first bank of Shawneetown.

posed against some of the early money problems in pioneer southern Illinois.

These problems were brought about by several factors, particularly by the absence of "hard money" on the frontier. Silver and gold coins were so hard to come by in those early days that Spanish milled dollars, called Pieces of Eight, were legal tender in many southern Illinois frontier banks.

As one historian reminds, a southern Illinois bank, lucky enough to obtain two silver dollars during a day of hectic banking, put them on display as curiosities so rare was the event.

To provide a medium of exchange, for trade or barter, banks had to issue their own currency such as the odd-denomination notes from the bank at Old Shawneetown, mentioned here.

These "shin-plasters" were issued in many denominations no longer in use today. The notes were supposed to be backed by "hard" money, silver or gold, but frequently they were not. Many of these early banks issued as many as four and five times as many notes as they could redeem in hard currency. Some of these beautifully engraved bills also were issued on banks that never even existed, an out-and-out fraud. Today, these "counterfeits" are highly prized by numismatists all over the land.

Merchants, of course, were hardest hit by this type of money. When offered in trade, they could never be sure whether it was the real thing or fictitious. Even some of the legitimate notes had to be discontinued.

So bitter became the competition among early banks that one institution would gather all of the currency it could on some other nearby bank, then present it in a bundle, in an attempt to "break" the competing firm.

The bank at Old Shawneetown survived several of these "runs" on its currency by one of its rivals, the Bank of Edwardsville, about a hundred miles distant. Later the two banks patched up their differences and began sending each other's notes as far distant as possible, in an attempt to stabilize their own economy.

The U. S. Government finally ended this wildcat currency by issuing a federal bank note, which was slow in being accepted, viewed with suspicion by many, but finally able to stand on its own merits.

The sheaf of odd money shown here was photographed in the recently-opened Docker Historical Museum at Old Shawneetown. Howard Mayes, one of the curators, proudly shows the sheet of old bills in possession of the museum. Include Old Shawneetown and the Docker Museum in your itinerary the next time you tour southern Illinois. You won't be disappointed.

From Dogwalk to Pinch

Did you ever visit the Devil's Bake Oven, at Grand Tower, Illinois? Or whizz through the tiny community of Dog Walk, also in the southern part of the state? Perhaps the Washington County community named Pinch struck your funnybone. Or have you wondered, after reading a road sign, Crooked Creek, whether or not the stream was actually crooked enough to warrant the name? They all exist, as do hundreds of other unusual place-names tacked onto cities, towns, creeks and rivers in Southern Illinois.

Music, humor, romance and irony, are all concealed in the place-names we give to sites in southern Illinois. Why? There are various reasons.

Long ago Robert Louis Stevenson said: "The names of the states themselves form a chorus of sweet and most romantic vocables . . . there are few poems with a nobler music for the ear; a songful, tuneful land, and if the new Homer should arise from the western continent, his verse will be enriched, his pages sing spontaneously, with the names of places that would strike the fancy in a business circular.''

Have we forgotten the American Indian in southern Illinois? Not by a jugful! Memorials of our plains Indians, now extinct, are found in such place-names as Mascoutah, Buffalo, Cahokia, DeSoto, DuQuoin, Makanda, Tamaroa, War Bluff, Indian Gap, Shobonier, Patoka and numerous others.

And how we've "borrowed" from the Old World: Paris, Pulaski, Vienna, Karnak, Thebes, Waterloo, to name just a few.

We even remember our own statesmen. Washington County is one of no less than 169 places within U. S. borders that bear his name; 86 are named Jefferson; 132 Jackson, 71 Monroe. All four have their counterparts in southern Illinois.

There are oddities in place-names here, too: Sailors home from the wars settled in the community that is now Marine, in Madison County; Alma in Marion County goes back to the great battle at Alma in the Crimea; the Swiss settled Highland, once referred to as Helvetia; the mountains of Palestine figured in the naming of Lebanon; Sparta was named for the ancient Greek city; Odin owes its name to a god in Norse mythology. Countless southern Illinois churches answer to old-world names such as Zion, Ebenezer, Joppa and Mt. Olive.

Now-vanished Santa Fe in Alexander County was named after the Spanish town of the same name in New Mexico; General John B. Turchin, "the Mad Cossack" of Civil War fame, settled in Washington County and named the village he laid out as Radom, from his native Poland. Tonti in Madison County was named for

La Salle's man Friday of the same name. Southern Illinois' Beaucoup Creek, and the village of Beaucoup in Washington County, were named by the early French; LaClede in Fayette County, traces its name back to the French founder of the city of Saint Louis, and so it goes.

Many southern Illinois place-names were hand-me-downs, borrowed from the Bible, literature, history and even mythology. The Kaskaskia River, now being canalized for industry, owes its name to a once-powerful Indian tribe who lived here; the Ohio is still the "beautiful river" of song and story, named by the Indians who lived on its banks; the Wabash was "shining water" to still other area tribes.

The village of Pinch, now being incorporated into the Okawville community, got its name from Plum Creek, a line of demarcation between the two communities; often the creek flooded and put the villagers "in a pinch," hence the name.

Sometimes southern Illinois place-names are deceiving. The Big Muddy River, for instance, isn't any muddier than the Kaskaskia or the Wabash. Rattlesnake Creek might have been the home of reptiles in the dim past, but talking to people who live in its basin today reveals there are very few snakes left.

Most of the place-names of southern Illinois have been part of the area's geography for long, long years, unchanged. But once in a blue moon a place-name grows so obnoxius that it is updated. A fishing stream in Hillsboro County, New Hampshire, originally was mapped as Quohquinapassakessamanagneg. No wonder it is shortened today to Beaver Creek!

The "Andersonville" of Illinois

A recent cleanup program on the Mississippi riverfront at Alton, uncovering an old wall from the debris of years, has brought a grim story of a smallpox epidemic into sharp focus.

The old wall, ready to topple, is all that is left of the first State Prison built in Illinois, often called the Confederate Pen or the pest house.

The century-and-a-half old wall, all that remains today of this infamous prison of Civil War days, was buried under debris, vines and creepers, literally forgotten. Once the debris of years was cleared away, there it stood, a grim reminder of wholesale death during the war between the states, a black page in early Illinois history.

Built in 1830-31 and known as the first state prison in Illinois, it soon became the center of violent controversy that eventually ended in a legislative investigation and the construction of a new prison upstate at Joliet.

Badly situated in a low spot too near the Mississippi, undrained and ungraded, it aroused the insistent criticism of Dorothea Dix, pioneer in prison reform. With the outbreak of the Civil War, the plan to discontinue the prison's use was abandoned and it became a military detention camp, filled with Confederate prisoners, many of the young soldiers little older than boys.

Overcrowding and lack of sanitation facilities soon culminated in one of the worst smallpox epidemics ever to occur in southern Illinois. The time was 1863. The disease raged for weeks uncontrolled for want of prison doctors.

Prisoners died at the rate of six to ten daily!

The citizens of Alton became so alarmed that at last they demanded the stricken men be taken to a nearby island in the channel of the Mississippi River to protect the townspeople. Here a deserted dwelling was converted into a "hospital".

The unnamed sandbar in the river soon was known as Smallpox Island, due to the many deaths there.

No evidence exists today that any of the soldiers ever returned to the mainland alive! Although no records of deaths were kept, it has been estimated that several thousand persons died and were buried there during the war years of 1863-64. Those who were not buried on the island were interred in a plat in upper Alton, known today at the Confederate Soldiers' Cemetery. A tall obelisk there tells the chilling story of the smallpox epidemic.

After the war, the prison was evacuated, sold, and the buildings razed. But ironically one wall, for some reason, was left standing. And it remains today, ready to topple but still a wall, shorn of its vines and debris, a grim reminder of a black page in the nation's history. A historical marker has been erected there by the state, telling the grim story.

An out-of-state tourist, looking at the ruin, smiled grimly. "This could well be another Andersonville," he said. "It's odd that some writer hasn't told the story in depth."

It would be easy to agree. Here soldiers died by the thousands when a smallpox epidemic struck. The killer epidemic itself was caused by the filth allowed to accumulate by the officials who ran the prison. No death records, apparently, were kept, or if they were, are unfound today. But somewhere in the South, parents grieved for a boy who died here.

Stand quietly if you visit the spot, and perhaps you will still hear the moans of the dying on the wind.

Obelisk with a Chilling Inscription

In Upper Alton, to the west of Highway 67, the story of the smallpox prison continues. Here stands the tall obelisk that Altonites refer to as "the Smallpox Needle." For a tablet on this granite shaft reads: "In memory of 1,354 soldiers who died of smallpox."

In today's age of antibiotics and vaccination, this many deaths attributed to a killer disease seems almost unbelieveable. Yet when these incarcerated soldiers died, slightly more than a century ago, smallpox and other "plague" type diseases ravaged unchecked because no one knew how to check them.

Standing at this obelisk today, the tourist sees historic proof of death because of man's carelessness. These young soldiers died because of indifference and callousness on the part of others. It takes little imagination to envision the heartache and despair of loved ones, living far distant. There was no television to dramatize the deaths in one's living room, but the pangs were just as keen.

Time erases and mellows all things, but site of this old prison wall, the island in the Mississippi, and this green hill in Upper Alton with its tall obelisk, brings it all back into sharp focus. These men were the Kennedys, the Kings, the Evers of yesteryear, and we've forgotten all about them!

A Pioneer Burial Ground

"For miles and miles it is all Miles'."

The man who made that statement has long been dead. His body is in the ruins of a fifty-six vault mausoleum that stands at a lonely and seldom-visited spot on the brink of a limestone escarpment known as Eagle Cliff, in Monroe County, about eight miles north of Valmeyer.

The sprawling Miles' Cemetery -- or what remains of it after vandals have wreaked havoc with the century-old stones

and a large mausoleum -- is being restored by the archaeological department of the Monroe County Historical Society because of its pioneer background.

The spot might be hard to find for the stranger, but it is well worth a visit. If one is coming north from Valmeyer on the blacktop road that hugs the foot of the cliff, or south from Columbia along the same road, the large mausoleum can be seen atop the cliff from the floodplain below. Once you sight the mausoleum, look for a T-road, one all-weather lane leading upward through Dug Hollow, a good climb but easy for modern cars. Once you're atop the bluff, turn right, and soon you'll see the cedars along the rim of the cliffs, marking the old cemetery.

Despite the vandalism, the cemetery has been used as late as 1963, as attested by the stone atop the grave of Mrs. Anna Wright. One of the oldest burials in the cemetery is that of Elijah Axley, who was born in 1798 and died in 1853.

There are several hundred graves here, plus the 56 vaults of the Miles clan, inside the mausoleum, and vandals have left very few standing.

Entry was also made inside the mausoleum, where coffins were opened and desecrated. Now cement slabs have closed the openings created by the ghouls.

But on a visit to the cemetery in recent weeks, this writer found that one of the cement slabs sealing the mausoleum had been hammered until an opening was made large enough for human entry.

What are the ghouls seeking? Buried treasure within the ancient crypts? Jewelry buried with some of the corpses? Whatever they seek, the vandalism is deplorable.

Stephen W. Miles was far from an ordinary frontier settler. Born in Cazenovia, New York in 1795, his education and culture was far beyond that of most of his compatriots of the day. He was a musical genius for one thing. The moment he came to southern Illinois, legend grew about him

The doors of the Miles mausoleum have been sealed with concrete, yet vandals keep battering it down to get inside.

and his followers, their intention to start a feudal empire in what is now called the American Bottoms.

Like the Rappites who settled at New Harmony, Indiana, Miles and his group followed the rivers to southern Illinois. Near Cave-in-Rock they landed and started the trek northwest until they saw the rich black soil of the American Bottoms. Here Miles prospered, and at one time owned thousands of acres of land he acquired in devious ways. So when he climbed the bluff to survey his "empire," it was only fitting that he would say "For miles and miles it is all Miles'."

But today Miles' empire has crumbled, and all that remains is the old mausoleum atop Eagle Cliff. An inscription on the large marble panel at the right of the walled-up doorway states it was built by Stephen W. Miles, Esquire, in honor of his father and descendants. It also states that the eldest son of each generation was to care for it, but the bankruptcy of the son disrupted the plan, according to legend.

Here is history, in ancient stone, lettered with hand chisels, honoring a family of pioneers, illustrating the truth of the poet Burns' assertion that the best laid plans of mice and men gang aft agley.

Part III
Of Man and Monuments

The Cross of Peace

Some men dream, and let the dreams die; other men dream and make the dreams come true by hard, arduous work and a tenacious spirit. Retired mail carrier Wayman Presley is that kind of man.

Four miles from the small southern Illinois community of Alto Pass is a bare-topped mountain, part of the Ozark Chain, called Bald Knob. It is the highest spot in the area and commands a breathtaking view.

Upon its top today, seen from distances as great as fifty miles, is a huge 111-foot-high white cross, sheathed in gleaming white porcelain and floodlighted at night, one of the most elaborate shrines in the nation.

It was built, literally, by the efforts of one man, retired rural mail carrier Wayman Presley of nearby Makanda.

The "dream" started back in 1937 when Presley and a close friend, Rev. William Lirely, walked through the valley one quiet evening. Presley pulled up, pointed to Bald Knob.

"What a spot for a huge white cross!" he said.

Lirely at the moment presumed his friend was joking. But Presley was serious. He believed it could be accomplished, and immediately started to promote the idea.

Followed years of work, of exploitation, of disappointment. Then Presley got a breakthrough. He appeared on the national TV show, Ralph Edwards' "This is Your Life!" The publicity of the telecast brought Presley more than 300,000 pieces of mail, most of which contained donations for the cross.

Today, as everyone familiar with southern Illinois knows, the huge cross is an actuality, a symbol of one man's belief in an idea. It is called "The Cross of Peace," and at least one airline points it out to passengers as they fly over. At night, with its 40,000-watt floodlights turned on the gleaming shrine, it is reminiscent of a fine painting. It also is the site of an annual Easter sunrise service that draws people from a wide perimeter.

Physically, the huge shrine has been constructed to withstand gales up to 150 miles an hour. It is all steel and concrete, sheathed in porcelain, anchored to bedrock. The cost is more than a quarter of a million dollars, and most of it came in small sums, out of the goodness of the people. Sometimes dreams are wonderful things.

Work still to be done on Bald Knob at this date includes landscaping the mountaintop, and updating the four-mile road to the top of the mountain.

Giant Rend Lake

Imagine a lake with nearly 19,000 surface acres, a shoreline of one hundred and sixty-two miles. That's giant Rend Lake!

Started in June 1966, already Rend Lake is updating a vast area in southern Illinois. The two-mile long earthern dam that impounds the Big Muddy river near Benton is viewed with awe by the visitor seeing it for the first time. The particular thing about water impoundment here is its relation to the Intercity Water System, part of the Rend Lake Conservancy District, allowing forty-four separate communities, all in the perimeter of the lake, to use its treated water.

This is something brand-new to the area, where there are many small communities and once-prosperous towns now feeling the brunt of a decadent coal era. Many of the people living here have not had water facilities outside of their own private wells and cisterns. Rend Lake changes all of that.

Under contract arrangement, Illinois will pay the Corps of Army Engineers $8,100,000 to provide a maximum gallonage of 40 million a day for a fifty-year period. The conservancy district will reimburse the state.

Rend Lake will also attract a potential two million visitors annually, starting with the third year after completion, officials believe. As one planning executive stated: "It's like dumping $400 million into the economy of a region that needs the crutch."

Rend Lake College, with a new campus near the lake, already is a bright new image.

By way of comparison, Rend Lake has a dam 10,600 feet long. The dam at Lake Carlyle is 6,570 feet. Further upstream, Shelbyville dam impounds the upper Kaskaskia with a dam 3,025 feet in length.

As rivers go, the Big Muddy in relation to the Kaskaskia is rather an insignificant stream, so small that at the end of a long summer drouth one can wade across it in various spots. It is narrow, sluggish and as its name implies, quite muddy. In wet seasons, however, it turns into a flash-flood type of stream, inundating thousands of acres of farm land in its wide, flat basin. It is an erratic, prankish river that wends through the eroded coal lands of several southern Illinois counties on its way south to empty into the Mississippi near Grand Tower. But now it is harnessed, and the giant lake back of the dam is little short of amazing.

New Interstate 57, a major north-south highway, runs very close to the east side of the lake, even crosses several of its fingers. Already, Inland Steel Company has a modern "contained" coal mine on the north side of the lake. Other industries are coming in, as well.

Geographically, Rend Lake reservoir is a three-fingered body of water extending northward from the dam near Benton through Franklin county into Jefferson county. In the center wedge of the two big fingers nestles the village of Nason. The mayor of the community hopefully sees an upswing in the economy of the region and perhaps a revitalization of his town.

Already outdoorsmen are interested in Rend Lake as a potential paradise for fishing and wild fowl hunting, a sprawling family recreation area with wide appeal, offering a new lifestyle to many.

Our Lady of the Snows

There was a period in history when only Europe boasted great religious architecture. But now southern Illinois has added a shrine so noteworthy and beautiful that it is duplicating and even surpassing many of the finest on the continent. Such a shrine is the constantly expanding Our Lady of the Snows near Belleville.

It ranks as one of the largest outdoor Roman Catholic shrines in the nation. It is the only one dedicated to Our Lady of the Snows, incidently. Established by the Oblates of Mary Immaculate, it has attracted people from every country on the globe.

Sprawled on a rolling, 200-acre site atop the bluffs of the Mississippi River flood plain, just off Illinois 460, floodlighted at night, the shrine is noteworthy to young and old, regardless of creed or religion. One of the outstanding sculptures at the outdoor altar is a ten-ton statue of Mary, as Our Lady of the Snows.

The sprawling shrine includes a replica of France's famous Lourdes Grotto, a unique motor highway, "Way of the Cross," a huge altar with a ciborium of unusual design, and an amphitheater that can be expanded to seat as many as 20,000.

Angelus bells set in an unusual reflec-

As many as 20,000 people can worship at this outdoor shrine at Our Lady of the Snows.

ting pool use the water's surface as a sounding board. The four bells, cast in Germany and obtained from a Chicago church since torn down, are electrically operated. They are activated several times each day and can be heard for a distance of twenty or more miles. In the Spring, this pool is lined with tulip beds, so gorgeous when in bloom that visitors come in droves.

The origin of the Catholic veneration of Our Lady of the Snows dates back to 352 A.D. when, according to tradition, a childless Roman couple wishing to express their love and devotion to Mary, consulted with Pope Liberius.

He advised them to pray for a sign and, according to the legend, the Virgin appeared in a dream to both the couple and to him, asked that a church be built in her honor where snow should fall that night.

Snow did fall that night -- August 5th -- on the crest of Esquiline Hill near Rome, and there the basilica of St. Mary Major was erected.

The Lady of the Snows shrine near Belleville was suggested by the Rev. Paul Schulte, famous as the "flying padre of the Arctic," when he visited Belleville during World War II days.

The shrine began as a drawing and a few candles in the seminary chapel of St. Henry's College at Belleville, but soon outgrew these quarters as the Oblate Fathers' novenas, special devotions and prayers began to attract wide attention.

The outdoor shrine began in 1958. Workmen are still at work, creating new housing for the elderly, etc. The bulk of the money for this multi-million dollar enterprise came in the form of small gifts from the people.

Today, the shrine has its own powerful radio station, and is a mecca for Christians from all over the world. In these troubled days of tension, revolt, the generation gap, they come from all directions. They are hungry, and here their spiritual appetite is appeased. They go home with happy, relaxed faces. Such is the power and magnetism of this commanding shrine.

Population Center U.S.A.

Southern Illinois has a signal honor: since 1950 it has claimed the "U.S. Center of Population" marker, starting at Dundee, then dropping down to a site near Shattuc in 1960; lastly pinpointed to the Lawrence Friederich farm, between Mascoutah and New Memphis in 1970.

It all started back in 1790, when America was a colonial youngster. The first population census was taken. At that time, incongruous as it may sound today, the first population center of the nation was 23 miles east of Baltimore, near Chestertown, Maryland.

In the 183 years since that time, the "center" has traveled westward more than 725 miles, dipping slightly south in the process.

Today the new 1970 population center is less than 30 miles from the Missouri border, so southern Illinois could very well lose it in 1980, if present population trends continue.

The new census center is 727 miles west and about 45 miles south of the first marker dating back to 1790. Down through the years people have been following Horace Greeley's advice to go west. Seemingly the trek never stops.

The population center moved to Virginia in 1810. Fifty years later it had crossed to Ohio soil. Kentucky got it in 1880, then for the next sixty years Indiana claimed it, incidently a longevity record by any one state.

In 1940, the last year in Indiana, the site was near Carlisle. By 1950 the result of heavy industrial development on the west coast shot the center across the Wabash River to Dundee, Illinois, near Olney, a shift of 42 miles westward and 7.5 miles south. From Dundee the center moved to Shattuc, near Centralia in 1960. Now it is still further west.

The population center is described by the Census Bureau as the point at which an imaginary flat, weightless and rigid map of the United States would balance if weights of identical size were placed on it so that each represented the location of one person on April 1, 1970, the last day of the current census.

The nation's geographic center is in Butte County, South Dakota. One other geographical marker claims attention in the nation -- Four Corners Monument, where the states of New Mexico, Arizona, Utah and Colorado touch. Southern Illinois can be justly proud of the publicity it has received through its three census markers.

Until 1980, the Mascoutah area will have an enhanced tourist image, for the census obelisk set on the front lawn of the city hall there is a mighty magnet to the curious.

The Railway Giants

The city of Centralia, always a railroad town, has a permanent image of steam, in "Old 2500," one of the largest of the Illinois Central coal-burning locomotives, now put to pasture in Fairview Park there. From the time the Illinois Central "loaned" the big engine to Centralia, it has been mounted on its own track alongside Highway 161, a vivid reminder of the age of steam, so precious to the older railroad buff.

It was quite a feat to move the big mogul across town from the Illinois Central spur, a mile distant. Track had to be laid, taken up and laid again. After the engine got to the park, old railroad buffs stood night guard for nearly a month, until a hurricane fence could be built to protect it.

Since the engine has been in Fairview Park, it has been repainted no less than four times, to keep its image spic and span. In that time, nearly 100,000 children have been taken up into the engine's cab.

As an attendant explained to a visitor: "The engineer froze in the winter and boiled in the summer, but the age of steam was a romantic one that never will be forgotten."

Admission to the locomotive is free, and it is open to the public from 2 to 4 p.m. daily with the exception of Mondays, or during inclement weather.

Old 2500 was one of the largest steam locomotives on the Illinois Central, pulled the crack passenger trains during its long years of service. Its immense size is only realized when one climbs up into the cab, or stands alongside its drivers. It consumed coal and water in copious amounts; its whistle was a plaintive moan that once heard was never forgotten.

To the west of the engine is a granite marker, placed there in honor of a Centralia Illinois Central engineer, Robert T. (Polecat) McMillan, who before his death had reached national acclaim, due to the fact that he rode an Illinois Central coal-burning engine as engineer until he had reached the age of 83, traveling more miles behind the throttle than any other living man.

There are other references to steam in southern Illinois, an old switching engine mounted in a riverside park at Grand Tower, and several freight engines used as work horses in mine yards. But Old 2500 at Centralia is the shining image of steam at its finest.

For the Freedom of the Press

Today we are so hurried, travel so fast that often we miss things at the side of the road. But the Lovejoy Monument in the city cemetery at Alton is so tall and outstanding it commands attention from afar.

It marks the last resting place of Elijah P. Lovejoy, first American to give his life for "the freedom of the press."

Elijah Parish Lovejoy, eldest son of a Presbyterian minister, was born at Albion, Maine on November 8, 1802. He was a precocious youngster, and could read the Bible fluently when but four years of age. After college, young Lovejoy taught school in Vermont, then felt the call of the frontier and emigrated to Missouri. At St. Louis he taught school during the day, contributed to the city newspapers in his spare moments. Later he served as editor of the **St. Louis Observer,** organ of the Presbyterian Church.

His new work gave him voice. Soon he started a crusade against drunkenness and intemperance of any nature. He considered slavery an evil, was bitterly opposed to it, yet was not classed as an abolitionist.

He made enemies, and as time passed, his vitriolic pen crusaded bitterly against the slave movement. At last he was advised to move on -- for his own safety.

Finally he took the advice of friends, moved his printing press across the Mississippi from St. Louis to Alton. The day was Sunday, July 24, 1836. Because of the Sabbath, Lovejoy let his printing equipment remain on the wharf. His enemies took advantage of the incident, dumped the press and his type cases into the river.

Lovejoy promptly purchased a second press; it was sabotaged by a mob, who warned him of his life.

Undaunted, Lovejoy acquired a third press -- and it met with the same fate. Before a new press arrived to replace it, Lovejoy appeared at a meeting of his enemies and vigorously defended what he called the "freedom of the press."

Five days later, the new press was stored in the riverside warehouse of Godfrey, Gilman & Company. As rumblings of mob vengeance spread throughout the city, a Company of Militia went to the warehouse, presumably to guard the newspaper equipment. Lovejoy was among the guards.

The mob gathered, attempted to burn the building. Gunfire erupted and one of the mob was killed. As a second attempt was made to burn the building, Lovejoy came outside, to beat out the flames. He was fired upon and killed.

Thus Lovejoy became the first martyr in the United States to the cause of a free press. He was buried on the bluff the following day, incidentally his thirty-fifth birthday.

Later, when a new road was laid out, it was found that Lovejoy's grave was on the right-of-way. The same Negro who dug his first grave was commissioned to dig a new one, in the city cemetery. The body was removed to its present resting place, beneath the high granite shaft erected in his honor.

Lovejoy's death, perhaps more than any other single event, gave impetus to the abolitionist movement.

The Lovejoy Monument is easy to find. Follow Highway 3 through lower downtown Alton, turn north on Monument street and climb the hill to the city cemetery. It is southern Illinois' most imposing tribute to a man who believed in a cause.

The Lovejoy Monument is southern Illinois' most imposing statue to a man who was dedicated to a cause.

The Cathedral of the Prairie

One sees the tall twin spires of St. Charles Borromeo Catholic Church long before the tiny hamlet of DuBois, sprawled at its feet, comes into view. Unusual as it may seem, this giant cathedral-like edifice in southeast Washington County, its value surpassing half a million dollars, is surrounded by a town little more than a hamlet.

Often called "The Cathedral on the Prairie," St. Charles Church has been visited by people from every state in the union and many foreign countries. Reminiscent of some old-world church, its twin spires rise 116 feet, and dominate all other buildings in the area. The brick edifice is 131 feet long, 80 feet wide, 58 feet high. A combination of Roman and Byzantine architecture, its pictorial windows are art treasures of rare beauty.

St. Charles Church towers over tiny DuBois like some giant. The interior of the church rivals some of the greatest metropolitan cathedrals. About 200 Polish families in the farm area surrounding the church are its mainstay. At the time the building was started in 1908, local people and the clergy all helped buck a saw and swing an axe in its construction.

DuBois is French. But there are no Frenchmen here. The community is predominantly Polish, with an infiltration of German. In fact, the community has two names. On the Illinois road map it is listed as DuBois. But until the Illinois Central depot was torn down, the railroad called it, simply, Bois. The name was shortened, rail officials said, to avoid confusion with the next stop to the south, DuQuoin.

Until the DuBois coal mine was closed, it was called Illinois' oldest mine. The mine at DuBois was sunk during the same time that Lincoln was freeing the slaves.

Although there was no electricity in the mine, it was considered safe, and during a century of operation, but two men lost their lives there. One was killed when a powder blast went off prematurely; the second was scalded atop ground when a steam line broke. Mules pulled the coal cars below ground.

The mine had a romantic history. Located alongside the Illinois Central railroad tracks, it witnessed the passing of the old balloon-stack locomotives, the "iron horses" of Civil War days. Its first coal fired some of the famous Hayes ten-wheelers before the advent of the diesels. Casey Jones, railroad immortal, steamed by the mine on the road's high iron.

DuBois was first called Coloma, a tight little group of ten Polish-Catholic families. In 1874, due to the Prussian Kulturkamp in Europe, Poles seeking escape from religious persecution imposed upon them by the German chancellor, Bismarck, emigrated to the DuBois area in considerable number. A Negro community once located here has entirely disappeared.

The Poles, even today, predominate. Such names as Kyscki, Kania, Wyeiskalla, Mossa, Ruziewski, Zyk, Nikrant, Ezperra, Psyska, Malkowciwz and Grezechowiak, are found on the rural mailboxes. Until the turn of the century, Polish was the mother tongue here.

A proud hard-working people, deprived of their liberty in the old country, they took the clay hills and marginal land of this Southern Illinois area and made them into attractive farms.

Motorists traveling U. S. 51 can't miss DuBois, because of the height of the twin spires of St. Charles Church, an image of togetherness in a tiny southern Illinois hamlet.

Part IV
Early Inhabitants

Uncovering the Past

The first buckskinned adventurers, trappers, traders and explorers, who came to the Mississippi Basin which later became part of southern Illinois, realized through many surface artifacts that primitive man had preceeded them. But the things they saw evidently were taken for granted. The various artifacts were disregarded, and little was set down in their journals. The mounds along the river's flood plain puzzled these men, but nothing more.

But today, man's curiosity is writing a factual history of the primitive peoples long dead. We might be a bit late in amassing this wealth of cultural knowledge, but it is being done nevertheless.

As excavation work progresses at Cahokia Mounds State Park, between Collinsville and East Saint Louis; at Koster near Kampsville, and in the Fort de Chartres area, further south, new light is being thrown on this giant river culture that faded into dust more than a thousand years ago.

All of the digs are different. At Cahokia, the excavations concern the giant mound itself, trying to find its ramps and outward fortifications; at Koster, the dig concerns ancient villages, one on top of each other, long buried; at Fort de Chartres, both Indian and early French artifacts are sought. Each has its own purpose in our culture.

If you talk to the young archaeologists working at Cahokia, you might hear the story of a chief so powerful that he was buried on a blanket decorated with thousands of mother-of-pearl shell beads in the shape of an eagle, surrounded by six attendants, all killed to accompany their master into the other world. You might also hear the story of the sacrifice of 54 young women buried in one grave and a second pit containing 21 more skeletons of young girls. You might also learn that the Indians who built the mounds have been called Mississippian because their culture first appeared along the river between Cahokia and Memphis. From these village sites the Mississippians developed large scale corn and vegetable agriculture, a system of towns which were the capitals of villages, a political hierarchy to oversee public works, and a religious culture that produced the many mounds, plazas and art.

Southern Illinois' pioneer settlers had many legends and stories about these mounds, the Cahokia chain in particular. One legend has it that the builders of this giant earthwork chain were a lost tribe of Israel. Another described them as a people related to the Mayas and Aztecs. A third told of an ancient race, of much vision and beauty, with large cities and widespread commerce and trade, that flourished in the Mississippi Basin about the time of Christ.

Today, however, these myths have all been exploded. The mystery of the mounds has been solved. Archaeologists have been able to show clearly and positively that the mound builders were simply Indians who built mounds.

These earthworks were not all of one period, nor were they all built for the same purpose. Some were effigy mounds, others the sites for buildings.

Thousands of mounds are scattered through southern Illinois. The plow has leveled many of them. In the mounds are found obsidian from Yellowstone, catlinite from Minnesota, copper from Michigan, mica from the Alleghenies, and shells from the Gulf of Mexico. All of these things prove that the builders were nomads, wandering up and down the great highways of primitive travel, the rivers.

The Cahokia Mounds chain is part of the Mississippian culture. Their pottery is well made. Finely woven textiles are

The mounds in the Cahokia chain are many.
Monks' Mound, shown here, tops them all. Now
the famous mound is the site of annual "digs"
by archaeological students from various univer-
sities, intent on piecing together the artifacts
of an early culture that concentrated here.

frequent. The dwellings were square or rectangular. In the cemeteries near the mounds the dead were buried in extended positions, together with projectile points, pottery, charms and amulets.

Monks' Mound, largest of the Cahokia chain, is known throughout the archaeological world. Because it is protected in a state park, the diggers are in no hurry. They are taking their time, very methodical in their work. Monks' Mound, part of a chain that originally contained 85 smaller mounds, is the largest earthwork in the world. It's sad that so many of these lesser mounds were destroyed by man in his suburban sprawl. Luckily, the few remaining are on state property, protected.

Monks' Mound is a truncated pyramid, rectangular in form, with a broad terrace or apron extending from the south side; it covers 16 acres. Its greatest height is 100 feet; the east-west width is 710 feet and the north-south length including the terrace, is 1,080 feet. Here it is that the digs are currently taking place, an attempt to find the ramps that were part of the earthworks.

Looking at Monks' Mound today, still a giant earthwork, one is amazed that it was built. The herculean labor involved, men carrying baskets of dirt upon their backs, day after day, year after year, denotes either the existence of slavery or an almost fanatical religious belief. It was named by a band of Trappist Monks who, decimated with fever, camped near it in the long ago.

To the east of the mound proper is a recreated log palisade, built by the state several years ago, but somehow it seems out of place, too modern.

There is nothing modern about Cahokia. That is why it is such a charming place. For years men have been trying to sift the truth from the legends, and they are still trying, strengthening the true picture each time they turn a new spade of earth.

Give yourself plenty of time if and when you visit Cahokia Mounds State Park. Here primitive culture is coming alive. Visit the splendid museum with its many artifacts; walk up Monks' Mound, talk with the diggers; here is ancient history at your fingertips.

An 8,000 Year Old Campsite

Southern Illinois' newest archaeological marker is the culmination of experimental research that started back in 1952, when the bulldozer of a road-building crew unearthed a skeleton presumed to be that of an Indian, near the sandstone bluff now identified as Modoc Rock Shelter. The site is east of Prairie du Rocher, equally famous as a dig-site. A blacktop road hugs a long line of high sandstone cliffs here as it wends toward Modoc. On one side is this rugged line of demarcation, and on the other the Mississippi flood plain, stretching away to the river, four miles distant. Primitive man used the natural shelters of this cliffline for thousands of years. Now the site has been marked by the Illinois State Museum and the Illinois State Historical Society.

The inscription on the new marker reads: As early as 8000 B.C. prehistoric Indians were camping in the shelter of this great sandstone bluff. These nomadic people, who lived by hunting animals and gathering plants for food and fibers, came here regularly for more than 6000 years. Later Indian groups who began to settle in villages, used the rock shelter occasionally when hunting. The pioneers and their descendants continued to make use of the shelter in historic times.

Operation Rock Shelter started more than 20 years ago when a local road-building crew found a skeleton under the blade of their bulldozer as they excavated under a high rock shelter at the side of the road. Believing the skeleton was prehistoric, work was halted until archaeologists from Southern Illinois University could check the facts.

Suddenly everyone was excited. The skeleton was Indian. The archaeologists realized an important find had been made.

"We're standing on an ancient camp-site," said Dr. Melvin L. Fowler, of the S.I.U. excavating crew. Very soon he proved he was right.

This shallow cave has since been cata-logued as one of the oldest dated sites of human habitation yet found east of the Great Plains. It compares to the recently excavated Koster Site and the Cahokia Mounds.

Once identification was made, it was easy to see why ancient man had chosen this spot as a campsite. The high cliffs were a natural waterbreak. Ancient trails ran here, both animal and human. So he camped here, buried his dead close to the sandstone wall. He hunted, ate the animals and birds he killed, threw away the bones.

This went on for centuries. And all of the time, wind-blown soil wafted over the sandstone wall, covered the ancient fires and graves, adding a foot or two of loess each century.

When the dig started here, Fowler and his crew believed they would find arti-facts as deep as 12 or 15 feet. But their estimates were too conservative. They went down 26 feet, to bedrock. And all of the way down, they uncovered arti-facts.

One of the choice finds was the skeleton of a teen-aged girl, buried in a sitting (flexed) position, with the knees drawn up under the chin. Age of the burial was estimated at 8000 years. Other prized arti-facts were turtle-shell bowls and pro-jectile points. Radiocarbon tests of char-coal samples in the cave indicated that human habitation was present here in 8000 B.C., after flood waters from a melting glacier receded. Occupation con-tinued here through various prehistoric cultures until about 1200 B.C. Tests of pollen found here showed a very hot and dry climate in Illinois at that early age.

Dr. Frederick Matson, then of Pennsyl-vania State College, visiting the site, recovered charcoal from different levels of the dig. These specimens in turn were processed by the Institute of Nuclear Studies in Chicago to show their age which was determined by radioactive matter still within the samples. The scientists found that charcoal taken from the 15-16 foot level dated back to about 4000 B.C. The 21-22 foot level was 2200 years older, and the lowest levels of the dig showed an age dating from over 9000 B.C.

Not only do these findings make Modoc an important site but it also identifies this sandstone bluff as one of the oldest sites of habitation of Archaic peoples who lived here at the same time the famous Folsom peoples were in the west. In fact, primitive man camped at Modoc when the last of the great glaciers still covered southern Canada. So it is highly ap-propriate that Modoc Rock Shelter is permanently marked.

To find the spot, if you come in from the east or south, turn off of Route 3 at the Roots junction, and continue west through Modoc. If you come in from the west, con-tinue through Prairie du Rocher, angling west on the blacktop road until you come to the site.

Modoc Rock Shelter is only one of the things to see in the area. This is a vast archaeological graveyard, following the river. There are many dig sites and if you proceed south, through Chester on Route 3, you'll see a large Hopewellian Mound on the south side of the road, near the Ava turnoff, one of several in the area.

The Piasa Bird

Southern Illinois' most famous Indian pictograph, a reproduction of the Piasa Bird, is losing its scales via peeling paint, on a limestone bluff wall north of Alton, facing the MacAdams Highway, part of the Great River Road.

The Piasa Bird, first repainted in 1924, then again in 1950, and reproduced at a new location in 1964, is practically obliterated today, but there is promise of another repainting in the near future.

Long a historical attraction on the cliff wall, the 1950 painting fell victim to progress when the MacAdams Memorial Highway was constructed. Evidently one of the first white men to see the original pictograph was Father Marquette and his crew when they passed by the spot in a canoe on "the great river."

The hideous-looking old bird, which according to legend once devoured the Miamis who roamed this area of southern Illinois, will no doubt live forever, even though weather and the patina of age is hard on today's paints.

No less an authority than the editor of **The Living Museum,** official journal of the Illinois State Museum, described the Piasa Bird as follows:

"In 1673, Father Marquette in his journey down the Mississippi saw a pictograph on the face of the rocky bluff near the present site of the city of Alton. He described it as representing two painted monsters which at first made us afraid, and upon which the boldest savages dared not long rest their eyes.

"They are large as a calf; they have horns on their heads like those of a deer, a horrible look, red eyes, a beard like a tiger's, a face like a man's, a body covered with scales, and so long a tail that it winds all around the body, passing above the head and going back between the legs, ending in a fish tail . . ."

There are two Indian legends concerning this pictograph on this eighty-foot-high limestone bluff facing the Mississippi. A Miami tribal tradition states that many years before the coming of the white man, two monsters with wings like eagles, alligator claws, and horrible voices (one sounding like a roaring bull and the other a screaming panther), lived in a cave on the Piasa bluff.

During a battle in which the Miami were engaged with the Michigamea, these two birds swooped down with horrible screams and each carried away a Miami chieftain, frightening the balance of the tribe so badly that they forever fled the Illinois country, not stopping until they had crossed the Wabash.

A second legend, an Illini tradition, tells that such a bird killed or carried off papooses, squaws and even braves. At last an Illini chief, Ouataga, went out to decoy the monster from its cave so his warriors could kill it with poisoned arrows. The monster at last came out of its cave, swooped for the figure of the chief, tied to a pole. Whereupon a hundred poisoned darts struck its scaly body, killing it. So the Illinis painted a picture of the bird-monster on the cliff wall, so all who passed could see the bravery of Ouataga.

Such is legend, two of many.

The sight of the pictograph evokes interest and curiosity in both old and young, and perhaps forever shall.

If you intend to drive the MacAdams highway, now completed from Alton to Grafton, to see the pictograph, wait until the news media announce the completion of a new painting.

This painting of the Piasa Bird on the bluffs near Alton is no more, due to highway expansion. The bird has been repainted on the cliffs further north, but this painting, too, is feeling the patina of age and needs to be redone.

Shaggy Beasts

Buffalo in 'Egypt?' Yes, there were many before the white man helped kill them off -- for profit.

There are still buffalo in southern Illinois, one herd in particular, owned by Oliver C. Joseph, Sr. at O'Fallon. The grazing range here is a pasture alongside a blacktop road that leads north from the city. A sign on Route 50 in downtown O'Fallon directs one to the site. There are good photo-taking possibilities from the side of the road as the herd grazes. But don't be foolhardy and climb the fence for a closer view. Even in a domesticated state, buffalos aren't exactly docile milk cows.

To some people, mention of buffalo (or bison) brings to mind memories of vast herds that once roamed the western plains, or a visit to Custer State Park in South Dakota, home of one of the largest buffalo herds in the nation. Like the now-extinct passenger pigeon, the number of buffalo west of the Mississippi River was once estimated at more than five million animals.

This estimate, bear in mind, was relative to animals west of the river. At an earlier age (before 1700) they were just as plentiful east of the Mississippi. But civilization came earlier here, and the vast herds were thinned out, finally to extinction.

The plains Indians, of course, slaughtered the buffalo. But unlike the greedy white man, they did not kill them wantonly. The animals were slaughtered for food only. Their hides were used for clothing and moccasins and other purposes.

The first mention of buffalo in Illinois is made by Father Marquette, who came as a missionary in 1673. His writings tell of seeing many of the huge animals on the plains near the river, as he headed downstream.

LaSalle, who came in 1680, wrote: "Far and near, the prairie was alive with buffalo."

That the shaggy animals were plentiful in southern Illinois as well as other areas of the state, is indicated by the fact that an early French trader named Juchereau established a trading post and tannery near the Saline River in southern Illinois about 1700 and collected 13,000 buffalo hides in a single year. Historians differ as to the trader's name. Some refer to him as Charles Juchereau de St. Denis. He established the fort and tannery by authority of the King of France. The slaughtered buffalo were killed solely for their tongues and hides as the herds came in to lick salt.

But such greedy and wanton work did not go unpunished, it seems, even at this early date. The workers at the tannery were massacred by the Indians. But the wholesale annihilation of the buffalo in southern Illinois already was so great that the herd never regained its former prominence.

One of the deep box canyons in Giant City State Park is pointed out as a buffalo trap, where hunters, both red and white, drove the animals to their death over the cliff.

John James Audubon, early naturalist, tells of buffalo in this area. The animals came in droves, lured by the many salt licks along the rivers, where many of them were slaughtered. By the eighteenth century, they were almost entirely gone from southern Illinois, yet even at this date, a Frenchman named Andre Michoux, traveling between Fort Massac and Fort Kaskaskia, recorded in his diary: "The 7th of October, 1795, my guide killed a buffalo, which he considered to be about four years old."

An old clipping from a southern Illinois weekly reveals the fact that the last

This is part of the Oliver C. Joseph herd, north of O'Fallon.

buffalo killed in southern Illinois was in 1808, but the source of this information is problematical.

Indian pictographs in southern Illinois show the buffalo, mute attest that the shaggy beasts were here long before the white man. The animal is also given mention in the folklore of the pioneer, both song and story. Unlike the passenger pigeon, the goliath of the plains will not be extinct, at least not in the foreseeable future, although the number of domesticated herds is low.

Buffalo tongue was once a delicacy of the pioneers and mountain men, superceeding all other meat. It took a special weapon, with an extra charge of powder behind its heavy bullet, to bring down the huge beasts, so the buffalo gun was invented. Presumably the weapon had the kick of a mule. At one time we had the beast on a nickel coin, now sought after by numismatists. And we will always remember William S. Cody as Buffalo Bill.

Part V
Where Illinois Began

Never a Volley from France's Folly

Ironic as it may seem today, the Republic of France once built a fort in the southern Illinois bottomlands near the Mississippi River, so elaborate and costly, that it came near sending France into bankruptcy.

And still more ironic, although this fort was termed "strongest in the new world," its ancient cannon never fired a single shot at an approaching enemy, red or white.

Some wag was at his satirical best when he stood back from the fort's thick stone walls to exclaim: "Never a volley from France's Folly!"

Such is the saga of Fort de Chartres, now partially restored on its same foundation walls near the French town of Prairie du Rocher, in Randolph County. Now the site of an annual Rendezvous, with several archaeological digs scheduled for sites nearby, the fort is attracting more and more historians and specialists intent on investigating and studying its unusual past.

An ironic hand seemed always to hover over Fort de Chartres. The first fort, built too near the Mississippi, was washed away in a flood. Rebuilt of logs, it was later abandoned as unpractical.

Jean Baptiste Saucier rebuilt it of granite in 1753, spending three years in the task. The new fort held a garrison of 400 men, had stone walls 18 feet high and 2 feet in thickness. Inside its walls was a storehouse, a guardhouse, a chapel, government house, coachhouse, pigeon loft, two buildings for officers, two barrack buildings, the (then) largest black powder magazine in America; kitchen, bake ovens, and four prison cells, all arranged to face a parade ground of twenty-one acres.

This was magnificence in the wilderness! Around the fort lived the Piankeshaws and other lesser tribes, augmented by the Iliniwek from the north. The cost of the fort: one million dollars, an amazing sum in 1720!

And the fort was never used for the purpose intended.

The Michigamis moved near the new fort for protection from their enemies, and soon clusters of cabins denoted new white communities: Belle Fountain on the bluffs; Sainte Anne, Saint Philip and Prairie du Rocher in the bottoms. Water mills were built at Cahokia, Kaskaskia and a windmill south of Fort de Chartres.

Imagine, in each direction miles and miles of wilderness, with Fort de Chartres as the hub of the wheel. The arched gateway was 15 feet high, and from a balustrade, bristling French cannon guarded the approach. (One of these cannons has been moved to a site near the well, where it is fired hourly during the rendezvous days).

But when the Treaty of Paris in 1763 ceded to England all that France claimed east of the Mississippi (save New Orleans), French domination in America was doomed. It rang the death knell to Fort de Chartres.

The French garrison held the fort until October 10, 1765, when English troops moved in and took possession. Renamed Fort Cavendish, it was the seat of British government in the Illinois Country until 1772, when it was abandoned and burned.

France's million dollar bubble was gone. The British marched out, and the primal forest gradually crept in.

The French had another dream of riches in the Fort de Chartres area that later turned to chaff. The limestone cliffs that were a line of demarcation here between the uplands and the Mississippi flood plain had long appealed to them as sources of treasure. So five hundred Negro slaves were sent in from San Domingo to mine the cliffs. But all they

The restorations at Fort de Chartres are all
authentic. Notice the massive chimneys, the
thick sandstone walls.

found was limestone. The slaves were eventually turned loose to shift for themselves, and many turned into local farmers.

Today Fort de Chartres is one of southern Illinois' finest state parks. If you have visited it recently, you probably came in via the back gate. The main entrance of today's restored fort is actually the back, or land gate, of the original fortification.

These early French lived in a water-dominated society. Everything depended on the river. All important travel was via canoe or bateau, and all incoming supplies came in via river, a journey of four months from New Orleans. All regional exports -- flour, salt, lead, furs and buffalo wool, also were sent out via river.

Land travel was by foot or by two-wheeled cart; horses were for the rich only. The one usable trail ran through Cahokia, St. Phillip, Fort de Chartres, Prairie du Rocher, on to Kaskaskia. The trail meandered through virgin forest or head-high prairie grass; it was gumbo mud during the winter and thick dust in the summer. Now Illinois highways 3 and 155 follow part of this original Indian path.

Today, Fort de Chartres has much to offer the historian and student. The big powder magazine is a heritage of early France. The well inside the compound is oldest in the midwest. The gateway, chapel, guardhouse and museum have all been fully restored, while the low walls of the lesser buildings are part of the spacious green lawn. To the stranger, the fort is astonishing: here is a bit of ancient France in midwest America.

Old Shawneetown Will Never Die

Many historic old river towns in southern Illinois have faded away, but not Old Shawneetown. Despite the ravages of the Ohio River, the establishment of a new town on higher ground to the west, Old Shawneetown clings tenaciously to life; old buildings crumble but new structures take their place; to the historian browsing its ancient streets, this is sacred ground, hallowed by many voices and incidents in the turbulent years of the past.

The first chartered bank in the young state of Illinois opened its doors on the banks of the Ohio river in Shawneetown in 1816. It was a prospering financial institution at a time when Chicago was still a swamp.

Now, the Gallatin County Historical Society is making a valiant effort to restore the bank to its frontier day appearance. But during the interim, the old building is slowly falling into decay. Literally, it is in danger of being carried away, brick by brick, by tourists and souvenir hunters. The ancient building, coming apart at the seams, is dropping bricks from its walls, one by one, its roof caving in. Tourists carry away the bricks as they fall, treasuring them as if they were made of gold.

John Marshall of Shawneetown, a pioneer merchant and trader, was the first man in the state to see the need for a banking operation. He organized Marshall House in 1813 as a private deposit and lending institution.

In 1816 he chartered the Bank of Illinois as the first official bank of the territory. The vault was a Kentucky oak barrel in a pit dug under the floor. The trapdoor was covered by a strip of carpet, and the cashier slept over the trap with a gun in his hand.

The bank became a federal depository for funds from the sale of land. It was allowed to issue notes to circulate as currency. This crude money (in odd denominations, such as three and four-dollar bills) was easily counterfeited and became a major problem in the area.

Shawneetown's Bank of Illinois operated until 1823 when federal funds were withdrawn. It settled with its creditors and

Illinois' first bank, hugging the levee at Old
Shawneetown, is to be restored. The building is
in a bad state of repair.

saved its charter for future use.

It began operation again in 1835. When the Second Bank of the United States at Philadelphia lost its charter in 1837, the Federal Government deposited $1 million in the Bank of Illinois, a momentous business transaction of the day.

However, this bank was liquidated in 1843, following the collapse of a state development scheme in which it was required to participate.

The sturdy brick structure resisted several killer floods, including the one in 1937 that came up to the second story. When the present levee was built following that flood, the old building was so close to the river that it barely escaped destruction.

Shawneetown is really a tale of two cities -- Old Shawneetown hanging on the banks of the Ohio refusing to die, protective levees on its riverfront, the main street lined with bars; and "new" Shawneetown, a modern mall-centered 35-year-old town three miles west on high ground, now the seat of Gallatin County.

It was the mighty Ohio and nearby salt springs that first brought Shawneetown to life, and it was one devastating flood after another that eventually sent its citizenry to higher ground. But some remained. They remain today, and have no intention of moving.

Old Shawneetown has seen the best of times and the worst. Those who remain there today live in a settlement of diverse images; tarpaper shacks and fine old homes now crumbling to dust. Take, for instance, the architecturally beautiful second bank, a classic building patterned after an ancient Grecian temple and erected in 1839 at a cost of $86,000. It's still fronting on Main Street, and across from it are the stone steps of a torn-down building where Robert Ingersoll, the famous iconoclast, once practiced law.

It sounds amazing today, but in 1810, eight years before Illinois became a state, the Congress of the United States authorized the establishment of a post office at Shawneetown to serve a vast wilderness area that now encompasses the states of Illinois, Indiana, Kentucky, Tennessee and Missouri. Because this post office was the oldest in Illinois it was chosen for the first-day issue of the Illinois Sesquicentennial stamp in 1968.

Although the Ohio was largely responsible for the birth of Shawneetown, salt as well played its famous and infamous parts in the life of the town. For many centuries Indians had processed salt from the salt springs on the nearby Saline river before the white man had penetrated this wilderness. The north part of Shawneetown is built on an Indian mound, while many others are located nearby.

The last Indians to live here were the Shawnees, peaceful woodland Indians driven from their homes in the East by the more fierce Iroquois, and it was from these Indians Shawneetown got its name.

Perhaps Shawneetown's most glorious moment was in 1825 when the Marquis de Lafayette, the French nobleman who assisted the United States in its fight for independence, stepped from a fine steamer, the Natchez, walked along a calico-covered path strewn with blossoms to the Rawlings House, later renamed the Lafayette Hotel.

Early Shawneetown was a rough town, as well, due to the many rivermen who lived there. A missionary visiting there in 1816 wrote that he found not a single soul who made any pretense at religion. But ten years later, a Presbyterian church was organized there.

This is historic soil. Browse long when you visit here.

Fort Massac

Describing Fort Massac, facing the Ohio at Metropolis (the town of Superman), seems to fall into the same category as Cave-in-Rock, further up the river: both places had an association with men good and bad in their past, and an assortment of legends and stories have a halo of historic romanticism in each instance.

Fort Massac, part of a state park now being upgraded with the building of a huge stockade and its blockhouses cornering the walls, is a legendary place, ranging from the abode of the great and near-great in history to the depraved.

And ironically, Colonel George Rogers Clark, a man who did very little for Fort Massac, perhaps spending a single day there in passing through the area, nevertheless adds lust and pomp to its historic past. Although the new blockhouse complex, soon to be opened, is south of the original foundations of the old fort, the statue of George Rogers Clark towers from its same pedestal, facing the broad Ohio as if guarding against some potential enemy.

There is a new vista here, as well. Looking south, one sees the nearly-completed four-lane highway bridge that carries Interstate 24 over the Ohio. Clark, in his time, envisioned Indian canoes and keelboats, but never the high steel of present bridge construction.

The legends of Fort Massac date back to the early Spanish. The explorer, DeSoto, is said to have stopped here in 1542. But there is, of course, no documentary proof of this.

Father Mermet, a Jesuit priest, presumably preached a sermon here to the Indians in the Autumn of 1701 (or 1702), and because the time was Assumption Day, the fort was named Fort Assumption. More legend.

Massac's documented history begins in 1757. At that time, Charles Philippe Aubrey led a French force here, presumably to intercept an English invasion that never materialized. Aubrey, after scouting up the river for miles and finding no enemy, returned to the north bank of the Ohio where he built a temporary fort near the mouth of the Tennessee. Later the fort was rebuilt at its present site and named after the Minister of Marines, one M. Massiac. The French occupied the fort until the region was surrendered to the British in 1763. But the English did not occupy the fort, and later it was abandoned. In 1794 Washington ordered it rebuilt. The name was shortened to Massac, and again this stronghold on the Ohio was an important military post until its armament and stores were removed in 1814.

When the time eventually came to locate an arsenal in the Midwest, Fort Massac was seriously considered. However, after mounting political pressure, it was rejected, and Rock Island got the honor.

During the active years of Fort Massac, many historic names were connected with it, including Zebulon M. Pike, who later discovered Pike's Peak in Colorado; that cunning conspirator, Aaron Burr; the murderous Harpe Brothers of Cave-in-Rock fame; and the Indians, Tecumseh and Pontiac, to name just a few.

Today, the complete restoration of the fort gives it a new image. To anyone who browses here, sees the wide sweep of the Ohio at the fort's front door, it is easy to visualize its strategic location as a frontier stronghold. If those silent walls could speak, they would recite many deeds of honor (and dishonor) in the wilderness that later became southern Illinois.

The Second Liberty Bell

"May the filthy spot on which your Altars stand be destroyed; may your crops be failures, your homes dilapidated; may your dead be disturbed in their graves, and may your land become a feeding place for fishes!"

This curse, supposedly, was put on the southern Illinois village of Kaskaskia, first territorial capital of Illinois, by a bitter young Algonquin Indian who had been refused the hand of a French maiden in marriage. The prophecy probably is the creativity of a white man, long dead. Even so, it all came true.

The Mississippi River at extreme flood stage in the Spring of 1881 did destroy the frontier town of Kaskaskia. It tumbled the village church into the muddy flood, brick by brick. It inundated the growing crops of the French farmers, unearthed their cemetery, exposed many of their dead. Lastly, the river created a new channel, seven miles to the East. And in so doing, formed a 14,000-acre island. Today, the site of the original town of Kaskaskia is in the mainstream of the half-mile-wide river, "a feeding place for fishes." The new village of Kaskaskia is on the island created by the flood.

In the belfry of the colonial Catholic church was a bell, removed before the waters claimed it, since grown quite famous. Today it is called "The Liberty Bell of the West," posing an assumption that there is not one, but two, Liberty Bells in the nation.

Statistically, this is true, for in 1778 the Kaskaskia Bell rang out the joyous news of George Rogers Clark's capture of Kaskaskia for the Commonwealth of Virginia.

Two years before, on July 4, 1776, the Liberty Bell at Philadelphia had rung out the signing of the Declaration of America's independence.

So in reality, the nation **does** have two Liberty Bells, a fact that has had little publicity because of circumstances. The bell at Philadelphia is famous; the one on the tiny island of Kaskaskia is enshrined in such an obscure location, geographically, that it is almost unknown except locally.

Of the two bells, the one at Kaskaskia is older by eleven years. It was cast at La Rochelle, France, in 1741. Etched in the bronze in French is the following inscription: Pour Leglise Des Illinois. Par Les Soins du Roi. (A gift of the King, for the Church of the Illinois).

The Philadelphia bell, like the one at Kaskaskia, is cracked. The Kaskaskia bell weighs six hundred pounds, while the one at Philadelphia tips the scale at two thousand. The island bell is rung each July 4th. But since 1835, when the Philadelphia bell cracked while being tolled for the death of Chief Justice John Marshall, it is no longer rung.

Kaskaskia islanders insist that a crucifix was dropped into the molten metal when their famous bell was cast in France, an act of consecration. Whether or not this is true is debatable. Be that as it may, the history of this bell is little short of amazing.

In 1776, an English visitor to Kaskaskia described the community as being well built, the houses mostly of stone quarried from the nearby limestone bluffs at the edge of the river's flood plain. But from that date the town declined. The culprit was the river. Floods in 1785, 1844, 1851 and 1875 did great damage to both village and farmside. Then in 1881 the Mississippi again swept over the bottomlands and the town, engulfing the smaller Kaskaskia River in its mad race southward. The village of Kaskaskia was doomed. On the night of April 18, 1881, the Mississippi "gobbled up" the smaller Kaskaskia, so to speak, the death knell of the town.

Later, when the flood receded, the Mis-

The Kaskaskia Bell, 11 years older than our
Liberty Bell at Philadelphia, as it appears to-
day, enshrined in a tiny chapel on Kaskaskia
Island, part of Randolph County, Illinois.

sissippi remained in the other river's bed, seven miles to the east. The old channel of the Mississippi was nothing more than a sluggish creek. Fourteen thousand acres of land had been turned into an island by the breakthrough.

What remained of the battered town, on a precarious point at the head of the newly-formed island, lost more and more of its ground as the water continued to eat away the gumbo banks. Several buildings were moved to safety, others torn down, still others slipped into the flood, including the church. But in the meantime its bell, a gift of the King of France, had been moved to safety.

The cemetery was a victim as well. Long years later, farmers plowing on the island, clearing new land, have uprooted tombstones that had been carried off by the force of the water.

The only artifacts relative to the old church, remaining today, include the bell, an altar stone of white marble, dated 1681; two reliquaries; a carved altar; six wooden candleholders; two small wooden statues, one of St. Joseph and the other of the Virgin Mary; and a water-soiled oil painting of the Immaculate Conception.

The most heart-rending moment of the town's submission to the river was the slow disintegration of the community cemetery. One moment a grave was exposed; the next it had disappeared into the yellow flood. History had turned a new page, quite violently.

It was the Jesuit Fathers who started the first mission here, integrated with an Indian village. Soon the settlement became a very necessary outpost in the Illinois Country, part of a thin line of civilization that stretched along the rivers from Louisiana to Canada.

Here, in a sweeping bend of the Kaskaskia, only a few miles from the spot where the smaller stream emptied into the Mississippi, the early French colonists built their village. The frontier community had a wide Commons as well as a fort. Virgin forest was cleared from the rich black gumbo for farm land. Oxen, with yokes attached to their horns by leather thongs, pulled the first plows that broke this rich sod of the Mississippi flood plain. "Barefooted" carts (absence of iron rims on the wheels because iron was not yet available here), rumbled through the streets.

The immaculate French housewives insisted that their husbands change to deerskin moccasins when they entered. Outside, they wore homemade shoe-packs. Kaskaskians thrived, danced, made merry. Somehow these early Colonials failed utterly to realize the potential fury of the nearby Mississippi.

A smaller river, the Kaskaskia, had often flooded their cropland. But after a few days the water always receded, and apparently was forgotten.

The new bell in the Church of the Immaculate Conception already was claiming its fame along the frontier. It had rung loud and clear when Clark and his mosquito-bitten band of "Long Knives" had snatched the frontier outpost from the British, liberating a territory so huge that today it comprises the bulk of five states.

The Kaskaskians were unusually proud of their church bell, remembering that it was a gift of the king. They remembered, also, the stupendous task of bringing it from New Orleans to Kaskaskia, strapped to a raft that was pulled upstream by men with handlines, working from the bank. Imagine, if you will, the hardships of these men who walked afoot through what is now seven states, following the circuitous path of the river, wading swamps, fighting mosquitoes, malaria and the elements, to bring the bell home.

It took more than two years. But arrive it did. Its toll from the church belfry was the first bell chime to be heard in the Mississippi Valley!

Upon arrival, the bell had been assigned to Louis Buyat, a figurehead in the village, who presented it to the Church of the Immaculate Conception in the name of its donor, King Louis XV of France.

And then the flood!

Today, the ancient bell is enshrined by the State of Illinois, in a tiny 20 x 30 foot brick building on the grounds of the new Church of the Immaculate Conception on the island. At last census, the village had slightly more than 100 people.

Most of them are of French descent, of Catholic faith. To the visitor, (the incomer as he is called), they converse in English, but within their own circle many revert to the soft patois of their mother tongue.

Kaskaskia Island itself is the only parcel of land west of the Mississippi River owned by the State of Illinois.

The bell shrine is visited by only a handful of outsiders, for geographically the island is so isolated that it is not easily found by the tourist. It is completely severed from Illinois. There is only one incoming or outgoing road, reached from the Missouri side, over a narrow bridge that spans the "old" channel of the Mississippi at St. Mary's, Missouri.

The islanders, natives of Randolph County, Illinois, must send their children to an Illinois school. The nearest is at the town of Chester, across the Mississippi. To get there, the children must be bussed over 11 miles of secondary blacktop Missouri roads to a toll bridge at Chester. There is not even a ferry from the island to the Illinois mainland. Living on the island itself is relatively safe today, for it is protected by levees. But its isolation is complete.

The islanders, separated from their native state and still a part of it, feel their isolation and neglect keenly. Theirs is historic soil. They have an equally historic bell. But very few can find it.

To those of you who care to visit the island, drive first to Chester. Then cross into Missouri via the toll bridge. Drive westward on Missouri 51 to a blacktop turnoff known as highway H (right turn). Follow H to its junction with Missouri 61 at St. Mary's. In downtown St. Mary's a small sign denotes the highway to Kaskaskia Island.

A Century of Terror

If a crime wave ever had its inception in the mind of man at one certain point in southern Illinois, it surely must have been at Cave-in-Rock, spectacular cavern on the Illinois side of the Ohio River in Hardin County. This huge riverbank cave at one time was the center of a crime orgy that is as gruesome and morbid as any tale to flow from the pen of Edgar Allen Poe.

Little do today's travelers and explorers, who come to the cave in ever increasing numbers, realize the terror of its 150-year-old past. All is serene today; the adjacent state park offers top camping and picnic privileges, with the "Beautiful Ohio" within sight. The story of this scenic riverfront would not be complete, however, without a dip into its past.

The story of Big Harpe, whose true name was Micajah, and his brother, Wiley, known as Little Harpe, make people shudder even today. Yet the incidents are factual, the characters real.

Law and order passed this spot in southern Illinois for a long stretch of time. Cave-in-Rock was a thieves' and murderers' hangout for nearly a century.

One Samuel Mason, an officer in the Revolutionary War, saw the cavern's possibilities when he chanced to visit the site. He was quick to decide that this was the spot to reap fame and fortune. Standing in the wide mouth of the cave, one

Even today, the eerie past of Cave-in-Rock is felt by the visitor who explores this giant cavern on the Illinois bank of the Ohio. For here, murder, rape and pillage went unchecked for nearly a century.

could see up and down the river for long distances.

Mason collected his henchmen, plus a bevy of harlots from the dives of New Orleans, and set up business in Cave-in-Rock. On the high granite bluff over the cave he erected a sign which read: "Liquor Vault and House of Entertainment. That was the bait for the keelboatmen who plied the river. Once they were inside the cavern, Mason's harlots soon got the men drunk, while their boats were rifled of their cargo and set adrift. No one ever lived to tell of the deeds. Operating thus, Mason's crime cartel continued, year after year.

He also set up a printing press in the cave, turning out counterfeit bills. When he found a boat crew too large or unruly to handle, he merely paid them for their cargo with bogus money and sent them on their way.

Physically, Cave-in-Rock is 55 feet wide, 20 feet high, with a depth of 108 feet. It was perfect for the job at hand.

Mason and his brothel got their first dose of trouble -- not from the law -- but from two brothers, Big and Little Harpe.

At the time, the two Harpes had joined a band of renegade Cherokee and Creek Indians in North Carolina, who had been banned by their respective tribes. These renegades were killers, but the two Harpe brothers soon showed them new tricks in brutality.

They dressed as the Indians did, in the untanned skins of animals they had killed. They were dirty, unkempt, with long, matted hair. Neither wore a hat, despite the weather. Big Harpe was a six foot giant, whose right name, Micajah, was never used. He was simply Big Harpe. His brother, Wiley, who was shorter, was Little Harpe.

When they heard of Mason's cave, they left the Indians, worked northeast. The first recorded charges against them was at Knoxville, Tenn. in 1798, where they stole livestock and raped several women. They were jailed but hacked their way to

freedom, killed a peddler named Payton. Enroute to the cave, they killed at least four other people, one a small boy named Johnny Trabue. At the mouth of the Saline river, in southern Illinois, they chalked up more murders, on a killing spree now that was sadistic and gory.

At Cave-in-Rock at last, they joined with Mason. But soon afterward, when they took a woman off a keelboat, tied her to a horse, and sent both the animal and its rider to their death from the top of the cliff, it was too much for even Mason and his men. The Harpes were ordered to leave.

Far outnumbered, the two brothers worked down-river, into Kentucky. When they killed a prominent Kentuckian's wife, they found themselves hunted by a large posse. Little Harpe managed to escape, but Big Harpe was killed, and his body hung alongside the trail for all to see. Even today, the place is still called Harpe's Head Road.

A queer coincidence dotted Little Harpe's life after his brother's death. He escaped the posse in Kentucky, but in Mississippi, in January, 1804, he killed a man on the road, only to find it was Samuel Mason, one-time king at Cave-in-Rock. Found guilty, Little Harpe was hanged near the present city of Greenville, Miss. on Feb. 8, 1804.

When law and order finally invaded the wilderness that encircled Cave-in-Rock, its century of terror came to an abrupt end. Today the State of Illinois calls it one of its finest state parks.

Several years ago, a Hollywood movie company was quartered for long weeks at the cave, using it, and the river, as locale for a major movie, "How the West Was Won." Local residents got to rub elbows with James Stewart and other Hollywood greats, including venerable Walter Brennan.

In his **Ohio and Mississippi Navigator**, a historical volume written by Zadoc Cramer in 1803, the bloody days of Cave-in-Rock are chronicled in all their bloodcurdling detail.

The crypt-like cavern has looked out on many crafts sailing past its door, the Indian canoe of the early red men; the keelboats of Mike Fink's days; and now the heavy river traffic that plies the Ohio as work boats. The delicate red columbine still grows from the limestone cliffs above the cavern, and the cave is much like it was back in those gory days when the lives of unsuspecting rivermen came to an abrupt end in its dark corridors.

The **S. S. Delta Queen,** plying the Ohio each summer, stops regularly at Cave-in-Rock, to let its passengers explore the cave's deep interior.

There are several caves in southern Illinois, but none quite meet the gory past of Cave-in-Rock. Charlevois, early French explorer, described it as early as 1744. So when you enter this cavern, and feel the dark, eerie grip of its infamous past, the feeling is justifiable.

Part VI
Ghost Towns

All that remains of McKinley today is this
old frame building, once a fourteen-room hotel.

Gone But Not Forgotten

Ghost towns have always intrigued the southern Illinois tourist. There are many. Some are entirely gone, with nothing left but the site itself. Others spawn unpainted buildings in a slow erosion of decay. The ghost town is not evidence of decline as much as that of change. Perhaps the town was in the wrong spot; civilization has moved on. Some of the towns have been victims of the river, such as Rockwood, in Randolph County. But the charm of a ghost town lingers on. Today one often sees the man with an electronic metal finder combing a long-deserted street, hunting for some elusive buried coin, or an old gun or other antique inside some ancient wall. There are oldsters, too, who still remember when the town flourished; they go back and sadly reminisce about the days of their youth.

McKinley Station is typical of many of Egypt's once-flourishing communities now sliding into oblivion. Located in southwest Washington County, all that remains today is a big, square building that was once a hotel. Hitchcock, viewing it today might well choose it as the site for one of his movies.

McKinley Station started as a dairy venture in 1894. The dairy farm itself was really a sprawling ranch well over a thousand acres. There were four large dairy barns and a creamery that stood west of the hotel. The town had the usual shops, plus this big 14-room hotel, which catered to urban folks who desired to spend weekends in a rural area. The Missouri-Illinois railroad had a flag stop here called McKinley Station, which gave the community its name. Urbanites who flocked to the hotel had saddle horses to ride over miles of woods trails, and indulged in various rural activities. The evening chores at the dairy farm included the milking of a hundred cows daily. The town grew as a spa, then the venture ran into financial mismanagement, and by 1905 a general decay had started. The Missouri-Illinois railroad still runs its traffic past the ghost town, but now the trains are thundering freights only.

Tourists who wish to see the site of McKinley Station should motor to Oakdale, Illinois, then take a blacktop road leading south from the town to the site. Or drive to Coulterville, and take a blacktop leading north from that community.

The Rise and Fall of Winkle

Coal has been the impetus spawning many a southern Illinois community, and the closing of a mine has been the death of the same town. Such is the saga of Winkle, alongside Illinois 13 in Perry County.

The houses here look shabbier, day by day. Paintless, they stretch along a road that was once Winkle's main street. One by one they are falling down.

But the few still retaining a roof and solid walls are occupied.

The rent (on an as-is basis) is eight dollars monthly.

No traffic noise, very little smog, no vandalism. Plenty of peace and quiet.

Only fly in the ointment, should you decide to pack up and move to Winkle, is the fact that all the houses have tenants, and no one intends to give one up.

The story of Winkle, between Coulterville and Pinckneyville, with route 13 on its south perimeter and the Illinois Central Railroad on its north, is the story of a once-booming coal town.

In the heart of southern Illinois' soft

coal belt, Winkle once thrived. The high steel tipple and higher smokestack of the Bald Eagle Mine were visible up and down the tracks. Grade of coal was excellent. The number six vein here was nearly nine feet in thickness! Biweekly payroll at the Bald Eagle topped $15,000. Miners were making money -- and spending it.

Winkle had the usual small town business block, a three-story brick hotel, a depot on the I. C., several good stores, a feed mill, barber shop, cafe, even a weekly newspaper, named after the mine, the **Winkle Eagle.**

Then the depression of the 1930s closed the mine. After a time, citizens of Winkle realized the hard fact that it would not reopen, so they started moving out. A salvage company pulled out all the saleable material from the mine, and the shaft was filled. Later the railroad pulled up its spur track.

One by one the business places closed -- all except the general store operated by Tom Goddard. Goddard said he was too old to move, so he would keep open the general store as long as he could.

But now Goddard is gone as well, and Winkle has no service business of any nature. You can't even buy a loaf of bread or a carton of milk there. Goddard had been a merchant there for 62 years. Today his big store is closed, slowly falling apart.

The houses in Winkle can't stand forever without repair. They were built at the turn of the century, most of them four-room structures, with no conveniences except electricity. The coal company owning the houses say they will rent them as long as they are liveable; when they pass that stage, they come down.

That's the trouble at Winkle. Nothing new, just the coal-blackened buildings, the pot-holed main street. Even Pop Goddard wore out in time.

Recently, however, Winkle had a boom day, the time Goddard sold out his merchandise. The big store, which once employed a dozen people, was full of ancient merchandise, much of it desired by collectors -- old bottles, button shoes, clocks, pictures -- from Castoria to primitives. Winkle was crowded that day. Then it was over. It's lamentable to think that soon the brome sedge that was once the prairie here will take over. Winkle will be just a memory.

At the Mercy of the River

Towns and communities usually are stationary -- but sometimes the streams upon which they locate for reasons of business or commerce, shift and move.

This is the plight of a once boom town in Randolph County named Rockwood.

Yellowed old documents in the hands of local residents there reveal that tons and tons of produce and "barrels of eggs" were shipped by steamer from the Mississippi river port of Rockwood back in 1857, when the village was hard on the banks of the river.

("Barrels of eggs" arches an eyebrow; if they handled freight back in 1857 as harshly as they do today, it could easily have been "barrels of omelets"). However, one informant insists the eggs were packed in sawdust and arrived without breakage.

Today, the Mississippi River, once at Rockwood's back door, is more than a mile to the south.

What remains of Rockwood today is a cluster of aging houses, a combination store and gas station, plus a tiny post-office, strung along Illinois Highway 3, about 7 miles east of Chester. Local

This restored house at Rockwood was part of
the underground slave movement. Slaves coming over from Missouri were hidden in the cellar
here until they could be moved to the next stopover, another old house at Eden.

78

residents point to an old two-story house, now restored, that once was a depot on the underground slave movement.

The town of Rockwood started existence as Jones Creek. Later its name changed to Liberty. (A large island in the Mississippi nearby, a stopover for Negroes fleeing slavery from Missouri, had the same name). Lastly the town was named Rockwood, its current name. A local citizen stated that the "rock" part of the name referred to the high rocky escarpment at the back door of the town, and "wood" was deemed appropriate for once this was one of the largest "steamboat woodyards" on the entire Mississippi.

Before the turn of the century, Rockwood wood dealers sold as much as $100,000 worth of "boiler" fuel to passing steamboats. No less a personage than Mark Twain refueled his boat here.

It sounds phenomenal today, but at the price current in that era, this meant selling more than a hundred cords of wood daily to the riverboats. There was ample wood at hand, of course. The three dealers supplying the steamboats employed a large group of men to provide the cordwood. Of course the chain saw was unknown then, and "bucking a saw" meant exactly that. Despite the hard work, the pay was usually less than a dollar per day.

Not only did Rockwood have a widespread image as a center for wood, a new steam flour mill also was built there on the riverbank in 1855, and went into operation the next year. Seven years later it had a disastrous fire. But the mill was rebuilt and produced as much as 250 barrels of flour daily, which was loaded to boats tied up at its backdoor dock.

A mill needed cooperage, so a cooper's shop was built north of the mill, on a rock ledge, and the barrels sent down to the mill in a chute. Some idea as to the mill's production can be obtained from the fact that at one time the cooper shop employed ten men to make barrels. At that time, flour barrel hoops were made from hickory saplings called hoop-poles. These were pliable shoots about an inch in diameter and at least seven feet in length. The pole was placed on a flat surface and held in place by a foot-operated clamp while the cooper used a drawing knife to shave away about half of the pole's thickness, thus leaving a half-circle hoop long enough to encircle a barrel. A lock was formed by measuring the length needed and cutting opposing notches in the edges of the hoop. These notches were locked together with the tapered end tucked under the hoop. When driven down, they held firmly in place. Now and then, one can still see this type of hoop used on small casks of herring, so-called gourmet food, shipped from Holland.

Then in 1885 a strange physical phenomena took place: after a flood, the Mississippi began to shift its course away from the town. Soon the mill went out of business for it had no loading dock. Now only the ruins of its brick stack and crumbling walls remain. The river is far to the south. Today the Missouri-Pacific tracks run where once the river flowed. The railroad came in 1903, but it failed to help Rockwood recover.

At the height of its pre-century glory, Rockwood had a commercial hotel, five dry goods stores, two groceries, 4 blacksmiths, a shoemaker, a dressmaker, a tailor, a plasterer, and no less than three physicians.

A furniture maker there (Tuthill) made such outstanding furniture that some of his rockers and chairs are still sought on the antiques market. Several Tuthill rockers are still in existence in the area, prized by their owners.

An underground stopping place for slaves escaping from Missouri into Illinois in pre-Civil War days, the restored two-story house shown here was one of several houses involved in the movement. On the north side of the highway, it is now privately owned.

Today, the Mississippi is almost out of sight, having shifted its channel at least a mile to the south. The tiny community still nestles under the high bluff wall where primitive man once camped, but the river has moved away. The rich black loam spewed up over a century by the shifting waters now grows record corn crops, but the new acreage spawned by the river as it moved southward also was the death knell to a town once an important southern Illinois riverport.

East of Rockwood, if you are lucky enough to find a guide who knows the area, is a site along the bluffs where even today one can see evidence of limestone cutting from the sheer walls. "The stone quarried here," the guide said, "was hauled to Waggoner's Landing on the river, then put on boats and taken to St. Louis, where it was used on Eads Bridge, then being built."

An Image of Yesterday

Some small towns telegraph their history as one approaches. There is no explanation of this statement other than the fact any reporter will vouchsafe its authenticity. Maeystown, quite isolated in Monroe County, is such a town. One comes down the steep bluff from the uplands to the floodplain of the Mississippi, and there nestled half in and half out of the rocky escarpment encircling a meadow is Maeystown. It could be Germany, Switzerland, the Gaspe Penninsula -- anything but southern Illinois.

Evidently Jacob Maeys had no intention of founding a town here; somehow it just happened. The time was the 1850s, and he set up a homestead in the meadow below the bluff. An immigrant from Oggenheim, Bavaria, Maeys had previously purchased a one hundred acre plat of land here called the McRoberts Meadow, part of a grant allotted to a Revolutionary War soldier. A spring of icy water gushed from the cliff at one end of the meadow, and he built a roomy log cabin here, then brought his bride to their new home.

With a partner, Jacob Pillard, he started a sawmill and named the meadow Maeysville. The venture seemed perfectly timed. Europeans were immigrating to the United States by thousands, trying to find some refuge that suggested the homeland. McRoberts Meadow got its share of the newcomers seeking homes.

Jacob Maeys suddenly found himself surrounded by other farmers, artisans and professional men. To name a few: Martin Fombauer, a stone mason; Jacob Hoffman, hotel owner; Heinrich Wippermann, tailor; Ludwig Alheim, a cooper; Carl Siebermann, wagon-maker; Ludwig Krone, shoemaker; Charles Wilhelm, physician; Peter Bickelhaupt, blacksmith; Heinrich Querheim, undertaker; Anthony Zeidinger, miller.

The immigrants kept coming in. Somehow the community's name changed from Maeysville to Maeystown.

A postoffice was opened in 1860, a rock church completed in 1867. By 1904 Maeystown had grown to 300, and a decision was made to incorporate. Jacob Jobb was the first mayor. A state bank opened, as well as a high school.

But by 1933 the swing upward had leveled off and started on the downgrade. The bank and high school both closed. Maeystown got caught in the trend toward the metropolitan centers. Many of its young people saw no future here.

Today, however, the people of Maeystown are more proud than ever of their old-world heritage, their unique community.

A picturesque old stone-arched bridge spans the creek flowing through the village. For a long time, there has been talk of tearing out the bridge, in a highway modernization program. But if they do, there will be resentment. The old bridge has been a mark of distinction for a long time in Maeystown, and many of the town folk want it preserved as sort of an image-status.

Here, where the culture was strictly German-American until World War 1, the feeling persists that the village should make no radical physical changes. It is good to live here just as it is, where the water of the creek that bisects the town is still pure and cold as it tumbles from one rock ledge to another. It's good to take a walk up the hill to the church at the crest, and still further to the cemetery, where the huge monolith marks the grave of the founder.

Maeystown has an image it desires to keep, not of bustle or prosperity, but of peace, serenity in isolation. Perhaps the younger people resent it, feel that they're bottled up, but not the older adults.

The motorist coming down from the bluff, should obey the "Slow!" signs, or he'll miss that arched rock bridge and land up in someone's turnip patch. The highway curves sharply to cross the bridge, then curves again. That bridge is an identification mark, and without it Maeystown's image would change.

Ghost Town on an Island

Southern Illinois, like most of America, has its ghost towns. But it has one that is distinctive if for no other reason it is located on an island.

The tiny French town of Pujol, located on Kaskaskia Island west of the Mississippi but under the jurisdiction of Randolph County, Illinois, is slowly being erased from the scene. The community that once boasted the large visitation of great numbers of people from St. Louis who came down-river to Pujol to buy food, produce and butter churned by French housewives, finds itself a victim of a mass exodus to urban centers.

Even so, Pujol today still has fifty-odd residents. But once it boasted five times that many. Its only church is shuttered, its one business place closed. The large brick building that once housed its grade school is a brick skeleton, its many windows the targets of vandals.

George Menard, long a citizen of Pujol, has an answer to the decay: "The farms on the island are all mechanized, needing less and less help; there is nothing for the young people to do here, so they move away."

That about sums it up. The twenty-odd houses at Pujol are mostly occupied, but there is no new construction, no updating. As long as a dwelling is livable it has a tenant, who enjoys the cheap rent, commutes to work elsewhere. Several of the old homes are quite elaborate, but slowly falling into decay. Hidden behind the levee, the community has a look of decadence about it. The streets are narrow, weed-grown; the only illumination after dusk are a few night-lights installed by individual citizens to give them a better feeling of security after dark. It's a historic place, but one can't live on history.

Down the blacktop road two miles is the larger town of Kaskaskia near the center of the 14,000-acre island.

There is an island cemetery near Pujol where both Catholics and Protestants residing on the island buried their dead. But now the protestant church at Pujol is shuttered and threatens to remain so.

Pujol already has the status of a ghost town, but one thing is certain: there were no ghosts in its historic past.

Part VII
Buildings and Bridges

Court House on the Bluff

Southern Illinois courthouses have been making headlines quite frequently, including Chester and Belleville's venerable buildings -- and now a third historic courthouse is making its bid for fame.

This one is located in the tiny town of Thebes, first known as Sparhawk's Landing, hard on the Mississippi River, in Alexander County. The brick and stone courthouse, sitting precariously near the edge of a high limestone bluff overlooking the town of less than 500 people, was built in 1848. The two-storied portico with its widely spaced but slender columns and dividing balustrade gives the facade the feeling of a very early and rather primitive Southern Colonial type. Edna Ferber used the building briefly in her novel, **Showboat.**

The Thebes courthouse is in a state of bad repair, but it isn't hopeless. Now the Thebes Historical Society is searching for documentary evidence that would be a fitting tribute to the building's past.

Legend persists that Abraham Lincoln practiced law here, if only briefly. A copy of the **Cairo Evening Citizen,** reporting on the court held in Thebes long ago, quotes from the case, thusly: "Then cometh the defendant, by his counsel, A. Lincoln, and moves that the case be dismissed for want of prosecution."

Once the seat of Alexander County, Thebes is located in one of southern Illinois' most depressed areas. If the courthouse can be saved, renovated and updated, tourism could give Thebes a much-needed shot in the arm.

Dred Scott, famous Negro slave, was at one time imprisoned in the dungeons on the lower floor of the courthouse, rumor persists.

Over the years, fires, carelessness, vandalism and decay have destroyed most of the records in the old building. Since serving as a courthouse, the building has at times been empty, been used as a school, church, lodge and for community purposes, including a city hall and village library.

Even without the records, the old courthouse has long been entrenched in southern Illinois history. Completed in 1848 at a cost of $4,400, the building served as the Alexander county seat until 1860. At that time the county's administrative center was moved to Cairo, then in its heyday.

Supposedly the courthouse was built by Henry Barkhausen, who immigrated to the United States from Prussia in 1835. Thebes is a town oddly arranged: half of it is atop the high limestone bluffs paralleling the river, the other half is in the flood plain of the Mississippi. Sitting on the veranda of the courthouse, one has a splendid view of the lower town and the Mississippi River at its doorstep.

Even though the courthouse has gotten little advertising as a southern Illinois historic landmark, more than 5,000 people annually find it, and tour the site. Traveling highway 3 southward, one turns off at the Thebes Spur, which leads to the historic building.

Presumably Egypt gave Thebes its name.

When Alexander County was established on March 4, 1819, five county commissioners were appointed to locate "a permanent seat of justice." They chose a new village site called America. But in a short time, the shifting channel of a river, plus business failures, turned America into a decadent community that soon entirely vanished.

Thebes Courthouse today, sits high on the bluff facing the Mississippi. Now a Historic Landmark, the old building once incarcerated the slave, Dred Scott.

The Kimsey-Roots house shown here, located near Tamaroa, was once part of the underground railroad that moved escaped slaves across southern Illinois.

Once a Haven for Slaves

If Mr. and Mrs. Calvin Ibendahl ever hear any ghostly sounds emanating from their home south of Tamaroa, it might well be the lament of Negro slaves once quartered on this huge 700-acre grain farm. The timbers and foundations of the ancient house hold more than a century of history.

Inside the walls here, presumably in a large (dry) cistern, countless slaves were hidden in the undergound trek from the south to the north. Known as the old Kimsey Crossing Farm, this homestead was built by the well-known southern Illinois educator, B. G. Roots.

Roots, an easterner, came to Perry County, Illinois in the early 1800s by way of the Shawneetown Trail. A strong abolitionist, Roots chose this area of southern sympathizers to carve a niche in history for himself and his family, despite threat of bodily harm.

Roots' first construction was a large log building where he immediately set up southern Illinois' first college, called the Locust Hill Academy. Soon he replaced the log classroom with a huge frame house. This second house had a definite place in Roots' abolitionist activities. There was ample room to hide runaway slaves, including the cistern.

Roots, among his many other interests, was a surveyor for the Illinois Central railroad during the 1830-40 era, and apparently took advantage of his position by furthering his anti-slavery activities. He had the tracks curved to pass over his property, also set up his own "private" depot, at which all trains stopped.

Slaves often disembarked from a train in Chicago, with no record of them ever boarding the train. The truth of the matter was simple: Roots loaded the slaves into empty freight cars when the trains stopped at his farm and they remained hidden until their destination at Chicago.

Most of the slaves quartered at the Roots home were escapees from Missouri. They usually crossed the Mississippi at Chester, were taken by hay wagon to an underground depot at Eden, finally to Tamaroa, thence northward via train.

Because of his friendship for slaves, Roots grew very unpopular in Perry County, and at one time a group of men planned to tar-and-feather him, but he found out about the attempt and quietly disappeared until the ardor of the mob cooled.

The slaves befriended by Roots were forever grateful to him, and many of them returned to the farm after the war, to work there until death. Some are buried in a timber tract nearby.

The Kimsey-Roots place has changed little since those hectic days. The old sandstone foundation of the house is still intact; the timbers of the home are well preserved. The sandstone foundation is an oddity, for there is no sandstone in this part of Perry County. So evidently the stones were hauled in by team and wagon.

Today, the house and farm is privately owned by Mr. and Mrs. Calvin Ibendahl, but anyone wishing to tour the historic home can make arrangements with the farm couple to do so. They are justly proud of their century-old home and its historic past.

William Jennings Bryan

One of southern Illinois' noteworthy statues, a bronze likeness of William Jennings Bryan, at Salem, is quite different from the hugh likeness of four United States Presidents cut into the granite of Mount Rushmore, in South Dakota, yet the same sculptor is responsible for both works of art.

The home of William Jennings Bryan now serves as a city museum in Salem, Illinois, birthplace of the famous American statesman. A monument of Bryan is located in a nearby park.

The late Gutzon Borglum is famous to millions of American for his "four faces on a mountain." But very few people realize that the statue at Salem is the work of the same man.

The statue of Bryan, gathering the patina of weather and age in Bryan Memorial Park at Salem was created by Borglum long before the giant Mount Rushmore presidential group was completed.

Yet Borglum's statue of Bryan has been in Salem only since 1961. Before that time it stood in Washington, D.C. but in 1960 a new bridge across the Potomac uprooted the statue, along with several others, and it was moved to Salem, Bryan's birthplace.

Millions of people drive to the Black Hills of South Dakota each summer to see Mount Rushmore. Perhaps many of these same people -- at least southern Illinoisans -- pass the William Jennings Bryan statue at Salem, little realizing that the four faces on the mountain were created by the same sculptor.

When Silas and Mariah Bryan went to Philadelphia in 1876, their sixteen-year-old son took advantage of their absence by going to St. Louis, where he attended the National Democratic Convention. He did not have a pass but induced a friendly policeman to let him enter via a window. Evidently young William was duly impressed by the political conclave, implanting the germ of statesmanship in his veins.

However, even considering his youthful enthusiasm, young Bryan could not have dreamed that twenty years later he would appear as a dominant figure at a similar convention, make a speech so powerful that it won national acclaim, as he accepted the nomination for presidency -- incidentally the youngest candidate of a major political party in the nation's history.

Born at Salem, Illinois on March 19, 1860, his birthplace home is still standing, stocked with the many mementos of his active political life. A lawyer, a politician, a speaker of great force, Bryan is known for his silver policy, and his "Cross of Gold" speech delivered at the Democratic National Convention held in Chicago in 1896.

Bryan never gained the presidency, but the life of the Great Commoner is etched deep in the pages of political history, and though his statue in Bryan Memorial park is tarnished with the patina of the elements, his image in the hearts of southern Illinoisans is just as bright as ever.

The Old Morrison Mill

Does an old pioneer mill hold a fascination for you?

The old Morrison Mill, a rambling frame structure in the village of Burnt Prairie, in White County, has been grinding corn for well over a century, using the same buhrstone that was purchased in France by one of the original owners. The heavy thirty-inch flint stone is eight inches in thickness, and seems impervious to wear. It must be cleaned and sharpened periodically, but outside of that, the stone seems indestructible. How many bushels of corn it has ground in over a century of use is problematical. If actual figures were available, it might be amazing, for this pioneer mill was used continuously by the people of the area over a long period of time, during an era when people depended upon a mill for their meal just as much as we use the supermarket today.

Milling in the Morrison family goes back to the early 1820s, when Andrew Smith settled near Pittsburgh, Pa., had his mill washed away in a flash flood. He followed it down the Ohio to Shawneetown, Illinois, but found the area so mosquito-infested that, fearing malaria, he came inland to the town of Liberty, later renamed Burnt Prairie. Smith was joined here by a young Scott named Peter Morrison, who later married Smith's daughter and became part of the family who owned a horse-drawn mill.

In the early days of White County, Liberty became one of the most important trading centers in a wide area of prairie. It was near the Skillet Fork River, then a deep, navigable stream. Steamboats made their way up the Skillet Fork to take out loads of produce, including whiskey and timber, all routed to New Orleans. Now the Skillet Fork, clogged with silt and debris, is little larger than a good-sized brook, except during the spring flood season.

Prior to the Civil War years, Liberty had a bank, a funeral home, four grocery stores, three pork packing plants, a cigar factory, a hotel, a mill, and a furniture factory. Now most are gone except the mill.

Marked by the state in 1967 as a historic site, the old Morrison Mill as it stands today did not originate in Burnt Prairie, but first stood in Enfield. Here it was dismantled, and each of the heavy timbers marked, then the building reassembled at its present location.

Usually pioneer mills are located on a stream, using water as power. But the Morrison Mill is not water-powered, but a steam mill. At one time it produced flour as well as corn meal.

Why was Burnt Prairie so-called? Local residents say the prairie here was set afire in early days by deer hunters. The wide expanse of this burned-over land suggested the name, Burnt Prairie, when the town changed its name from Liberty due to a mail condition.

To see this ancient mill, follow Illinois 45 south from Fairfield to a turnoff at Mill Shoals. Five miles on a good blacktop road brings one to Burnt Prairie. There is a large picnic park at the old mill, with fishing privileges in two lakes on the property.

The Illinois Iron Furnace

With much of southern Illinois suddenly in sharp focus in relation to coal, its gasification, and steel all booming the local economy, some writers already referring to the area known as Egypt as "The New Ruhr Valley," it might come as a surprise to certain readers that the smelting of metal is nothing new here. A booming iron furnace was operating in Hardin County back in 1837, the same year the county was founded.

Illinois Iron Furnace was the Pittsburgh of the area. It operated over a long span of years, its last fires being pulled in 1883, after forty-six years of productivity. Much of its metal had an active part in the Civil War.

The first smelting of iron took place near Hog Thief Creek, about four miles north of Rosiclare. Many records of this early iron furnace in southern Illinois were destroyed in a courthouse fire at nearby Elizabethtown in 1884. But enough remain, in different area sites, to tell the story of this primitive frontier furnace with factual sequence.

The first operator of the furnace was Chalon Gard and Company of Indiana. By 1872 ownership had passed to the Illinois Furnace Company, a corporation also chartered in Indiana.

Iron ore was obtained from large, shallow deposits found in the nearby Shawnee hills. Pits where this iron was mined still dot the area. Known as limonite, it was about half iron ore. Horse-drawn wagons hauled the ore to the fur-

Illinois Furnace today is the only historic restoration of its kind in the state. Located on Hog Thief Creek in Hardin County, once it furnished iron used in Civil War shipbuilding at nearby Mound City.

nace.

Today, the furnace has been completely restored by the state, to show today's generation how iron was smelted back in the days of the pioneers. The location is south of Karber's Ridge. Highway 34 leads down from the north, and joins Illinois 146, the east-west road here. Near the junctions of the two highways, you'll see markers directing one to the Illinois Iron Furnace on Hog Thief Creek. It isn't a major road, so drive slowly so you don't pass the modest turnoff marker. There are picnic facilities at the restored furnace site, located in a nice, grassy meadow. It's definitely a historical restoration you won't want to miss.

To fire the old furnace, charcoal was needed, so there were really two operations here. When the furnace was in full operation, about 1,800 bushels of charcoal were needed daily. The men who used native timber, cutting the same into cordwood, and then burning the same into charcoal, got the munificent sum of 4¢ per bushel for their product. Today that same charcoal would bring nearly fifty times as much.

During Civil War days, the pig iron produced by the Illinois Furnace was hauled by wagon to shipping points on the Ohio River, where it was used by the United States Navy Yards in Mound City, near Cairo.

Even today, it is not uncommon to visit a farm in Hardin County and have the owner display one or more of these old "pigs" smelted at the furnace. They were lost enroute, and ofttimes when the load was too heavy at Hog Thief Creek, pigs were thrown into the stream near the ford to lighten the load.

The restored furnace today is 52 feet in height. The round core (or lining) of the furnace in which the ore was melted is 8 feet in diameter. Old firebrick that lined this core have markings showing they were made in Pittsburgh. Graphics in a nearby shelter show the furnace in detail, explain how it worked. Steam boilers supplied the power needed for auxiliary equipment.

When the furnace was built, few of the natives possessed the skills needed in its operation, so key personnel was brought in from Pennsylvania, even Europe, to supervise the operation, while local men were trained for the job. A community grew up in the meadow across the road from the furnace, and was called Illinois Furnace. A post office was established in that name on October 2, 1846, with Charles T. Gard its first postmaster. The village grew and soon boasted the usual stores, a boarding house and several saloons. When the furnace closed, the village turned into a ghost town. Today, an old well is the only visible thing remaining.

Three miles east of here a simple name stone marks the site of the Martha Furnace, (1848-1857).

Tarry as long as you can at Illinois Iron Furnace. This is historic ground once trod by many Indian tribes; explore the hills and see the pits where iron ore was dug; walk the banks of Hog Thief Creek, and listen to the many legends concerning it. This is terrain that has changed very little.

Old Creole House

Not only are historic old courthouses being saved in southern Illinois, but this same "preservation fever" has spread to saving noteworthy old homes of historic worth.

In an effort to further preserve for posterity the culture of the early French in the Illinois Country, the Randolph Coun-

In the nick of time, the Randolph County Historical Society has taken on the project of restoring this old Creole House, remnant of French occupation at Prairie du Rocher. The house was built in the mid-1700s, according to records.

ty Historical Society has undertaken a new project in the nick of time: restoration and preservation of the old Creole House on the Brickey property in downtown Prairie du Rocher.

The old Brickey mansion, only home in southern Illinois to be built from the proceeds of a lottery ticket, is gone, presumably burned by vandals. However to the south of this site, part of the block owned by the heirs to this estate, is the old Creole House shown here, persumably built in the mid-1700s, long before Illinois became a state.

During the tenure of Harold L. Ickes as Secretary of State, the Creole House was recognized as having exceptional historic interest, and a plaque was issued by the Department of the Interior at Washington, D. C. to this effect. But no further effort was made at the time to preserve the old frame house.

The Randolph County Historical Society became interested in the preservation of the old French-built home when it was informed that the ancient structure was soon to be destroyed. The building has long been called the Creole House because it was built by descendants of the early French settlers of the area, known as French Creoles.

Although the exterior of the building currently is sheathed with weatherboarding, it is believed the frame is of uprights, consisting of corner posts and studs connected horizontally by crossties not unlike the rungs of a ladder. In this type of building, extensively used by the early French, timbers from local forests were often joined by mortises and tenons, then secured by wooden pins instead of nails. The roof at the time of building was of thatch, but later was replaced by conventional shingles. The interior walls were plastered and whitewashed (not painted).

The construction in the Creole House is said to be similar to that in many of the old French houses in Ste. Genevieve, Mo. nearby. Prairie du Rocher itself, proud of its French heritage, spoke the mother tongue quite fluently until the turn of the century.

A visit to the old cemetery here shows the predominance of French names, burials of white settlers intermixed with those of Indians and Jesuits. It is the only town in southern Illinois that annually revives its early heritage by a year-end celebration known as **La Guianee,** an event that has been celebrated there since 1722, when masked musical groups tramp the streets on New Year's Eve, singing the old songs of the motherland.

When restored, the Creole House will be another landmark in southern Illinois open to the tourist and historian.

The General Dean Bridge

Southern Illinois, with some of the most picturesque bridges in the nation still intact, also has another unusual structure, a swinging bridge that served as a river crossing for the last of the Conestoga wagons heading west in pioneer days.

With Illinois' huge man-made lake at its back door, Carlyle's swinging bridge over the Kaskaskia River is fast becoming a tourist mecca.

It's called the General Dean suspension bridge, now 114 years old. This old cable suspension bridge (the only one across the Kaskaskia, incidentally), was built in 1859. Its 35-foot-high towers support a span 280 feet long. The cables were rusting away and the towers crumbling when the bridge was restored in 1953, and the structure renamed the General William S. Dean Bridge in honor of the Korean war hero, a native of Carlyle, who spent

three years of his life in a prison camp there.

Grove Patterson, once editor of the Toledo, Ohio **Blade** was married on this bridge when he was a young printer on the Carlyle **Democrat,** adding to its distinction.

Once the bridge was the only area crossing of the Kaskaskia River on the St. Louis-Vincennes Trail, and its ancient boards saw the last of the Conestoga wagons on the trek west. In that day it was a toll bridge.

An old record gives the tolls as follows: single horse or male, 6 1/4 cents; sheep and hogs, 2 cents each; wagon and horse 25 cents; wagon and two horses 37 1/2 cents.

(There is only one irregularity in these toll prices. The United States never issued a one-fourth cent coin, although it did have a one-half cent copper coin. How did the toll taker make change of the 6 1/4 cent toll?)

When the suspension bridge was planned, a Pennsylvania man won the contract in the amount of $9,148, given on May 12, 1859. But ironically, when the bridge was completed, its cost had mounted to about $45,000, a momentous sum in those days.

The bridge served as a river crossing for 65 years. Then in 1951, Illinois Representatives Edwin Haag and Robert Branson sponsored a bill providing for funds to restore the rotting structure. Gov. Adlai Stevenson approved the bill.

On Armistice Day, 1953, General William Dean dedicated the restoration. Few among the almost 30,000 people in attendance, knew of the history and excitement connected with this fragile looking structure spanning the river at the old Goshen Road crossing.

A walk across this suspension bridge today can be an experience, especially if it's a windy winter day. One can feel rather than see the uncanny shiver and sway of the bridge, the protesting groans of the slender cables arching up from the bridge floor as the wind whistles eerily through the barren trees. If one is in the right frame of mind, you might even hear ghosts from the past slowly rolling their covered wagons over the bridge, or urging their reluctant livestock across the wooden boards.

In 1808 a wagon trail hacked out of the forest, known then as the Goshen Road, crossed what is now Clinton County. It extended from Edwardsville to Crooked Creek (now Centralia), then dipped southeastward to Walnut Hill, Raleigh and ended at Shawneetown.

In 1811, John Hill, the first white man in the area, erected a fort and established a ferrying service at the Kaskaskia crossing. The fort was made of logs, arranged in palisade form. Here assembled the Illinois Rangers, the settlers' protection against hostile Indians, most of them roving bands.

In 1816, Charles Slade and two brothers, Richard and Thomas, traveled to Carlyle and purchased Hill's interest in the ferry. Charles Slade became one of the most prominent men in the area. With a man named Hubbard he bought a general stock of goods and went into business on this new frontier. They were the first white merchants in the area.

In 1824, Clinton County was formed out of Washington, Bond and Fayette. In order to secure the county seat at Carlyle, Slade made a grant of 20 acres of ground upon the condition that the county seat be located here in perpetuity. In 1831 Slade was elected congressman to represent this part of the state.

One of Slade's sons, Jack Alfred Slade, became one of the west's first legendary gunmen, killing his first man at the age of 26. He was finally caught and hung by Vigilantes in Montana Territory during the Civil War. Even today, TV badmen play the role of Jack Slade in western dramas.

At least one settler was slain near the old bridge, a man by the name of Young. Presumably his body was buried about fifty rods south of the fort. The mother of the slain man, visiting the scene later, declared that she had sewed a large sum of money inside his clothing. For years after that, people dug to locate the body, but none succeeded.

Today, as visitors walk the old suspension bridge, they have a magnificent view of huge Carlyle Lake dam, upstream to the north. But few of them realize the historic impact of this site in relationship to a young, still unsettled state.

The Old Log School

According to the late John W. Allen, southern Illinois historian and folklorist, this one-room, log-hewn school house was the first institution of learning in the Carbondale area, now the focal point of a giant, ever-growing state university.

The schoolhouse was built in 1840, according to records unearthed by the historian. Formerly located east of Carbondale, it was moved quite some years ago to the grounds of the Lincoln Junior High School, perhaps ten blocks from Southern Illinois University.

Here the hundreds of students attending Lincoln Junior High enjoy their recesses in sight of the old one-room school building, perhaps little realizing the many advantages they have today, in relation to this dingy, one-window, one-door log building, whose sole source of heat came from an open fireplace.

The entire educational pattern of that day was far different from our present structure; due to muddy and often impassable roads, school districts were small, with one-roomers dotting the countryside.

Walking inside one of these pioneer schools today, one is amazed at the change; gone are the long, home-made recitation benches, the double desks; the painted blackboards, the pot-bellied stoves, the cluster of wraps and lunchpails stored in the anteroom.

Gone too is the water bucket and common drinking cup, the wall maps, the blackboard pointers and the dunce caps. Teachers of these schools were a stalwart breed of men and women. Grades ranged from one to eight. Spelling bees and box suppers were week-end social events in the one-roomers. Games of marbles and town ball occupied the time at recesses. Each student brought his or her lunch, perhaps a fried egg sandwich, or one of cold pork. Fruit was almost unknown in a child's lunch box. They came barefoot as long as the weather permitted, and often in midwinter the little tots dropped out for weeks at a time because of the rigors of the weather. The school bus still was unheard of, and walking a mile or more to school was the order of the day. Athletics was strangely absent in the one-roomers unless one included such games as whip cracker, Spanish leap frog, Indian rasslin' or bull pen.

Resembling an old pioneer school once attended by Lincoln, the tremendous logs used in this old building are still remarkably preserved, after 133 years of exposure to the elements. Fast becoming a tourist attraction, the building still is used occasionally as a setting for historic pageants or special classes, showing present-day students what school was like before the turn of the century.

The Church Without a Front Door

One of southern Illinois' most picturesque landmarks, the old Kornthal Lutheran Church, just off highway 127, three miles south of Jonesboro, is now open to the public as a shrine. Restoration work on the church is complete.

This unusual church was built by prot-

When Kornthal Church was built, there was
no front door, or steeple. These were added
later. Now the church is a state shrine.

estant families of the Lutheran faith who immigrated from Austria to America in the year 1852-53. Landing at New Orleans, these immigrants came up the Mississippi by flatboat to a spot called Willard's landing near the present town of Ware.

Traveling a few miles eastward they settled in a fertile valley which they promptly named Kornthal, meaning "valley of grain." The community was never incorporated as a village, but at one time consisted of a church, a church school and parsonage, a box factory, a grist mill, plus a store and a distillery. The church is the only remaining building.

The planning of the church was begun soon after settlement was made, and typical Austrian Betsaal (house of prayer) design was followed. Austria was then under Catholic domination and protestant churches were not allowed to have spires, nor were they permitted to have doors opening on the street. The new Kornthal church was a plain frame oblong structure with side doors and no steeple, 30 x 50 feet in size. The front entrance door, the steeple and bell tower were added in 1889. Even today, this building is known as "the church with no front door."

The interior of the restored church is impressive because of its unique design and the fine quality of its original workmanship. The pews were handmade of native yellow poplar, complete with kneeling racks. Balconies were constructed the full length of the building on both sides. A high pulpit placed the minister on a level with the balconies.

A stairway consisting of 12 steps leads to the pulpit and its guard rail is done in graceful wood filigree. Each step of the stairway represents one of the twelve apostles. According to legend, should any one of the steps collapse then that step is the one that symbolized Judas Iscariot. Over the pulpit is a carved canopy surmounted by a cross and containing a design representing a human eye which is symbolic of the "all seeing eye

of God." This type of pulpit is the same as one in Williamsburg and the one in George Washington's Church in Alexandria, Va.

Painted on the altar in German script are the words, Halte Im Gedaechtnis Jesum Christum, which in English means "Keep Jesus Christ in Memory." The white enameled baptismal font with its graceful lines, also was handcrafted by the builders of the original church.

Until 1923 all services were conducted in the German language and this practice, no doubt, contributed to the gradual decline of church membership. The church was closed in 1949. In 1953 it was reopened and services were conducted four times each summer under the direction of the Kornthal Congregational and Historical Society.

It became apparent, some years later, that the church was in danger of going the way of many historical structures, that of neglect and decay. After appeals were made, through various channels for its preservation, the State of Illinois passed legislation in 1960 whereby it acquired the property, repaired and decorated the building, and returned it to the newly-formed Kornthal Union County Memorial, Inc. in 1965.

So the old church lives on through the efforts of dedicated people. Today it is open to the public, and is also used occasionally for a funeral or a wedding. It is part of the rich history of southern Illinois.

House on Hickory Hill

Some old houses crumble and fall, others cling tenaciously to life. The "House on Hickory Hill," started in 1838 and completed in 1842, is in the latter category. Perhaps it is a tribute to its builder,

The Old Slave House atop Hickory Hill is a grim reminder of slave days in southern Illinois. The slave quarters are still visible.

John Calvin, that it seems indestructible. Or perhaps its illicit past adds to its longevity.

Not only is this mansion referred to as the House on Hickory Hill, it is also known as the Old Slave House. Its owner: John Crenshaw.

The architecture can be described as an adaptation of the Greek Parthenon. The first and second stories have colonnaded porches, while the third story forms of pediment above with a single large window at its peak. Even the laths were split by hand, and the nails handmade. Two 12 x 50 feet verandas are supported by 12 massive pillars, each 12 inches in diameter, cut from the heart of a pine. The house has an inner wall of brick covered with frame, a custom common in the East but rarely found in southern Illinois. A carriage drive pierced the house. It is now boarded up, but it would seem it was made for the express purpose of driving in a vehicle loaded with slaves, then unloading them behind closed doors.

Why the dungeons on the third floor, the whipping post?

Located on a high eminence, the old house is nine miles west of Old Shawneetown, overlooking the Saline River valley.

The image of this old house on the highest hill in the valley of the Saline is intriguing. Legend and fact are so intermingled that a true separation is impossible.

Lincoln is said to have stayed here one night. Perhaps he was conscious and concerned about that third story, with the dungeon and the whipping post. Who knows?

In an area where every man could hew out his own homestead and gain an independent living, the hiring of laborers was difficult. The government, recognizing this, permitted employers to lease slaves from their owners in slave territory and bring them to southern Illinois to work. Thus, John Crenshaw was allowed to lease large numbers of Negroes in

Kentucky and bring them across the river to Equality to work in his salt mines.

One of the most frequently told stories of the old house deals with Crenshaw's attempt to breed slaves and sell the young babies. For this purpose he imported a male Negro from the south by the name of Bob, whose record in begetting strong offspring was remarkable. Whatever the truth of this story, there still exists today a room on the third floor of the old house that is referred to as "Uncle Bob's room."

It seems quite likely that John Crenshaw yielded to the temptation to deal in the illegal practice of stealing slaves. The old house without doubt was part of the underground in this movement of blacks.

Crenshaw died in 1871 and his wife ten years later. A faded marker in the Hickory Hill cemetery marks their graves. The old house stands today, square and erect in spite of its aging years, the real monument left by John and Sinia Crenshaw. On the lawn east of the house one can see a large old beechnut tree, which was brought as a tiny cutting from George Washington's grave at Mount Vernon, and set out when the house was built.

Also in the yard are some of the old salt kettles used on the nearby Saline river in the days when Charles Juchereau de St. Denis established a tannery near Hickory Hill, slaughtered bison by the thousands.

Following the slaughter of the bison herd, came the commercialism of the natural salt licks on the river. Crenshaw moved in, took over the salt works, and sold the salt at a high profit. In fact, it was the salt that built the house on Hickory Hill. And finally Crenshaw turned illegitimate, it is alleged, and dealt in stolen blacks to add to his fortune. It was a dark image on the man who was a grandson of John Hart of New Jersey, one of the signers of the Declaration of Independence.

The old house was an infant during the

panic in Van Buren's administration; a fledgling during the 1849 gold rush, and well into its prime during the hectic days of the Civil War. It saw Lincoln's inauguration, and later his assassination.

Today, the visitor keeps asking: Why did Lincoln visit here? Was he interested in Crenshaw as an important figure in southern Illinois, or was he more interested in the third floor of the mansion, and the locked door at the head of the narrow stairway leading there? If the latter, did it strengthen his conviction to put an end to slavery? There are no factual answers.

But the visitors to the old house keep coming. Often they browse long, missing not a single detail inside the house or out. It has an illicit, compelling image. It also is one of the finest historic landmarks in southern Illinois.

The Covered Bridges

The State of Illinois at long last is taking a hard look at its eight remaining covered bridges, updating and restoring them for posterity, inviting both tourists and bridge buffs to visit them. Perhaps even now it's a bit late. Once Illinois had 132 covered structures; now there are only eight remaining.

The state had nine, until vandals burned the longest covered bridge in the state, located at Hamilton.

Southern Illinois, with only one covered bridge to boast about, can still shout loudly, for historians and tourists agree it is the prettiest and most photogenic in the state.

It is located in Randolph County, north of Chester, just off of State Route 150, and spans the Mary's River. This bridge, a burr arch structure 98 feet in length, was used as a toll bridge until the county

purchased it in 1872 as part of a toll road extending from Chester to Bremen. The single-land structure was used until 1930, when Route 150 was built. Now it is owned by the state, and has been fully restored, providing a fine picnic site for visitors.

It is the only covered bridge in the state that was once the scene of a murder. Photographers have dubbed it "The Christmas Card Bridge," because it has been thusly used so many times.

Illinois really has ten covered bridges, but two are listed as commercial. One, called the Sunshine Bridge, is in a park at Litchfield, Illinois; the other at Mahomet, built in 1965, spans the Sangamon River. It is topped with a shake roof, adorned with 28 windows. Purely a tourist attraction, the true covered bridge buffs do not recognize it for inclusion in the state's calendar of covered structures.

Other covered bridges in the state include what is known as the red bridge in Bureau county, near Princeton; one in Henderson county south of Oquawka; one six miles northwest of Douglas in Knox county, spanning the much-publicized Spoon river; the Greenbush bridge in Warren county; two in Sangamon county, one spanning Spring creek, and the other near Glenarm; the Thompson covered bridge in Shelby county, northeast of Cowden, the only bridge of this nature spanning the Kaskaskia River.

Until recently, the tourist had a difficult time finding some of these covered bridges, but now they are all marked.

According to a national magazine, Abe Lincoln is said to have used one of the covered bridges in Sangamon county as an emergency crossing, but there is no historical data to this effect.

Mary's Covered Bridge in Randolph County,
north of Chester, is the only one remaining in
southern Illinois. It ranks among the best of
the eight remaining in the state.

A French Colonial Church

Some scholar once remarked that to follow the history of a nation, first go to its rivers. This supposition is factual in many instances in southern Illinois. The earliest settlement, remember, was on the Illinois side of the Mississippi River. Illinois' first capital was on the river.

At Cahokia, which predates all other religious history in southern Illinois, the first log chapel was erected in 1699 by a group of missionary priests from the Seminary of Quebec, when they traveled south from Canada through the wilderness, following the rivers, to work with native Indians.

After the log chapel had served long years of usefulness at Cahokia, it was superceded by the Holy Family Church, built of hewn walnut logs, set upright to form a frame, as was the custom of these early French artisans.

Despite nearly two centuries of weathering, the ancient church today is in a remarkable state of preservation, to the amazement of construction men who have checked its timbers. The walnut logs are hard as stone; there seems to be no evidence of rot or decay.

Now at long last, this venerable church has been designated as a National Historic Landmark. On April 25, 1971, Bishop Albert R. Zuroweste of the Belleville Diocese, accepted a bronze plaque from the National Park Service, giving the church a new image as a historic landmark.

Missionaries of the Catholic faith and French explorers came into the Illinois Country together. The devoted missionaries came to convert the native Indians to Christianity. The explorers were of a different breed, seeking adventure and possible fortune. They kept moving on, establishing new frontiers, while the missionaries remained to establish missions and carry on their work.

Tradesmen, coming later, would often set up shop near some missionary outpost. Emissaries of the French Government did likewise. Thus it was that the early missions served a two-fold purpose, often being the nucleus of a community that later grew into a town or city.

One of these missions was Cahokia. Although the original log chapel and dwellings have long since crumbled into dust, the church that followed still remains. Amazingly, there are relics inside the church that date back to 1699. No wonder a continuous flow of tourists visit here.

Following the curiosity aroused by this ancient church of walnut logs set upright in its walls, a visitor today will soon find the patina of great age indoctrinating his thoughts. This is the oldest French colonial church still standing in the Mississippi Valley.

The ends of its vertical-set logs, hewed both inside and out, are mortised into other shaped logs lying along the bottom and top of the wall. The vertical logs have wide grooves in them, about two inches in depth, in order to retain the mortar and stones used to chink-and-daub the openings. The corners of the building are sturdily braced. The logs comprising the wall are staggered inward about eight inches, to better withstand the thrust of the roof trusses. These early French in the Illinois Country were carpenters par excellence.

The building's floor slopes gently, with a six inch drop from the entrance doorway to the altar. There is no ceiling. Bronze plaques and printed legends at appropriate places highlight some of the church's early history. Emblems used in the worship service of this and preceding churches

The Holy Family Church at Cahokia, built
in 1699, has weathered the elements for nearly
two centuries, with very little physical decay.
Now the church is a National Historic Monument. A constant stream of visitors visit it at
all seasons of the year.

and missions are distributed about the room. The old pews are gone, as are the charcoal foot warmers. Candles still burn at the altar.

In the quietness of the dim interior, it is not difficult to conjure up moments of the past: a motley group of worshippers, including solid French settlers and blanketed prairie Indians, with robed priests administering to all. This was a focal point for religion along the great river.

When the first mission was built here, at least two thousand Indians lived in its vicinity. Roving groups often camped on the open ground near the church.

It was at this spot that George Rogers Clark, after his conquest of the Illinois Country in 1778, conferred with various Indian chiefs in an effort to have them become friends and allies of the Colonists.

Back of the church, various old tombstones give credence to both Indian and white burials, side by side.

This is sacred ground. Now that the Holy Family Church has been given national recognition, it assures its permanency as an example of early Colonial culture in what is now southern Illinois.

Historic Cahokia Court House

Historians and tourists, seeking the old French courthouse at Cahokia often ask: "Where is it?" The historic French building, presumably built about 1737, sits alongside a narrow road, to the west of Illinois State Highway 3, almost totally screened from the motorist passing through.

Currently efforts are being made by officials of the equally historic Holy Family Church, located about two blocks east of the old courthouse, asking the State of Illinois to move the building to a site on or near the church property, to be part of the religious complex here that includes historic Jarrot Mansion.

Besides being on an obscure street that really is a truck route to eastside riverfront warehouses, this reporter has visited the old courthouse on different occasions when the building was locked, with no custodian present, denying inspection of the many artifacts inside relevant to the early French Colonial occupancy of the area.

Without doubt this is one of the oldest French-constructed buildings in southern Illinois, possibly the oldest private dwelling in the Midwest, and most certainly the oldest of all court houses west of the Alleghenies.

The old building is an excellent example of the French pioneer log dwelling with interstices filled with stone and mortar. The walls rest on a foundation of stone nearly two feet thick. The floors are of sassafras puncheons on walnut beams. It has four rooms, one of which was once a jail cell.

When erected, Cahokia was part of the French province of Louisiana. Marquette and La Salle failed to stop here, nevertheless it is the oldest permanent settlement in the Mississippi valley.

Named for a tribe of Indians, part of the Illinois Confederation, the word Cahokia signifies 'wild geese'. The 1723 census showed only 12 white residents here, but later it became the most populous of the French towns on the Mississippi River and had over 3,000 residents.

Because the old building was dismantled once and moved to St. Louis for exhibition at the World's Fair, then to Chicago, wags dubbed it "the galloping courthouse." It is one of four maintained in Illinois by the Division of Parks and Memorials. Moving once more, close to the Jarrot Mansion and the Holy Family Church, both shrines of their own, seems fitting.

One of the finest examples of early French
architecture in southern Illinois is the old courthouse at Cahokia, built in 1737.

Once there were grim devices of punishment on the grounds of the old courthouse, including stocks, a pillory and a whipping post. A unique feature of the Cahokia courthouse is its extended eaves entirely around the building, a feature common to early French construction. Many of the early French in Illinois came from the West Indies, where this type of construction was popular because of heat and rain. The French evidently liked the idea and incorporated it in their early buildings in southern Illinois.

The exact age of the courthouse will probably be forever argued by historians. One writer says it was built as early as 1716, a doubtful statement. It is definitely known that it was built by a Frenchman named Jean Roy Lapance for a residence, previous to 1790. The building later passed into the possession of Francois Saucier, who had married into the Lapance family. On October 8, 1793 Saucier sold it to St. Clair County for $1,000. From the time St. Clair County purchased the building, until the time the county seat was removed from Cahokia, it was used as a courthouse and a center for the military.

When the county seat was moved to Clinton Hill (now the city of Belleville) in 1814 the building was offered for sale. The purchaser was Francois Vaudry, who got it at a bargain, $225. From that time on, the building had rather a hectic existence, being used as a residence, a warehouse, and even a saloon.

When the structure was moved upstate after the World's Fair at St. Louis, it was reconstructed in Jackson Park at Chicago, and remained there so long (until 1939) that Chicagoans felt it was their own. But at that date the state acquired the building, and moved it back to Cahokia for reconstruction at its original site.

An old record tells about an open well on the grounds at Cahokia, into which a colt drowned. The pillory, the stocks, an old orchard on the grounds is no more.

But the reconstruction of the building is a notable job, well worth the time of a visit, if for no other reason than to study its unique architecture. The French were exceptional carpenters.

Part VIII
Links to the Past

Steam in Their Blood

Once the dog days of Autumn roll around, much of rural southern Illinois treats itself to a unique show: an Old Thresherman's Reunion held at the Pinckneyville Fairgrounds. The date always is in August.

Illinois, Iowa, Nebraska, Wisconsin, the Dakotas, Minnesota, Missouri, Ohio, Indiana, Kansas and Pennsylvania are some of the key states that have their annual shows, most of them held in late Autumn, when farm chores are at a minimum. The show at Pinckneyville is among them, rated one of the best.

You won't have trouble in finding the site of this old thresherman's meet once you get in the vicinity. A pall of black smoke hangs over the area, rising from the stacks of dozens of old farm threshing engines, going through their paces.

The Pinckneyville show lasts four days. (Watch the southern Illinois news media for announcement of the date). The ancient engines are put on parade, do stunts, and thresh grain at least twice daily.

The crowds love it, the urbanites equally as much as the rural folk. Children play in the strawstacks that form under the belching blower, and no one seems to mind the soot, or the blasting of shrill steam whistles.

At all of these reunions, the same general motif is followed: to show the present generation how the old steam threshing engine of grandfather's day operated.

All of the old engines on exhibit have "steam up," ready for a workout pulling a grain separator, a sawmill, or perhaps a veneering machine. Or possibly they simply chug-chug about the fairgrounds, giving children rides at two miles per hour.

The newly-threshed straw, clean and golden, laced with flying chaff, flows out of the separator's blower nozzle, to the amazement of today's younger generation. Only thing missing in today's reunions is passing the bottle and water jug, a tradition in grandfather's days. A few swallows of bourbon "cut the dust," followed by copious amounts of well water.

These old steam engines are expensive items for the collectors, but they don't seem to mind. First, they are scarce as the proverbial hens' teeth, growing fewer with the passing of time. Sometimes a hobbyist pays several thousand dollars for a choice engine, slick and clean, vintage of 1900 or even earlier. Possibly he spends another thousand to truck it home, and oftentimes suffers arrest from some alert highway cop for pulling too much dead weight over the existing highway.

Once the big mogul is in the back yard, they restore it, part by part, until it is in top operating condition, resplendent in new paint and all of the original insignia.

Many of these hobbyists belong to the American Thresherman's Association, or other state or national groups. The desire to preserve a facet of early Americana runs deep in these men. Most of the old engines were made before the turn of the century. Some of them today are valued collector items. And of course each has to be checked by a safety expert to see that the boilers are capable to withstand the steam pressure needed to perform.

It's a noisy show. The black smoke drifts in clouds, and tingles one's nostrils with an unforgettable pungency. Men and women take their turns at the throttles of the old steamers. Their rhythmic chug-chug, to an oldtimer, is a melodious sound unheard in today's petroleum world. This is the sound of steam.

A durable breed of machinery, the old steam engines are kept in the limelight mainly as a result of nostalgia. Back in

This 75 year old thresherman relives the moments of his youth as he looks at an old steam thresher.

Air pollution is given little thought at a meeting of old threshermen. The variety of old steam threshers all burn coal, and a pall of density usually hangs over the grounds.

The A. D. Baker, shown here, was one of the largest steam engines made. It was manufactured at Swanton, Ohio. This one is nearly 70 years old, and seems to be as good as ever.

the pre-World-War-One days, one long blast on the whistle of an old thresher informed the housewife that the crew were coming in for dinner (and that meant dinner at twelve noon, not eventide). And what a meal was served, a la smorgasbord, all one could eat.

Dangers of the old steam threshers included boiler explosions, leaking steam pipes, and always the possibility of a field fire from the sparks belching from the stack. Some of the old engines had hooded stacks for this purpose, but the sparks still flew under full throttle.

A thresherman doing custom work hired as many as thirty crewmen when he took to the road to serve a community. Generally the season started as soon as the first wheat was in the shock a few weeks, and continued until everyone was served. Often the cold winds of October fanned the crews on the last runs.

The ten-ton machines often were too heavy to travel over wooden bridges prevalent on most rural roads and lanes. So when the production of steam engines stopped in 1924, evidently it was a step in the right direction. But at that time, many famous names went into discard: Gaar-Scott, Keck-Gonnerman, Baker, Advance-Rumely, Buffalo-Pitts, Port Huron, Jumbo, Peerless, Case and Russell, to name a few of the more popular. The Jumbo, incidentally, was made by the Harrison Machine Works at Belleville, Illinois.

Even the "newest" of these steam giants is nearing 50 years of age. Many are 75 years old and still operable. No wonder nostalgia runs high.

In southern Illinois, this is grandfather's show, and he pulls out all of the stops to make it a success.

The Smell of Charcoal

Yum-yum! You inhale deeply and the aroma of steaks sizzling on the grill activate your tastebuds. Wood smoke, pungent sauces, and prime beef above the white-hot charcoal! No wonder barbeque cooking is so popular. But if it wasn't for the charcoal . . .

Perhaps you didn't realize that charcoal is produced in quantity in southern Illinois. One of several kilns in southern Illinois is located just off of Highway 149, west of Murphysboro, easy to visit.

Even today, actual charcoal burning is often a closely-guarded family secret, handed down from father to son. In the olden days, wood was stacked in piles, covered with earth, and ignited. But this is passe now. Most of today's charcoal kilns are built to specifications, made of brick, circular in size, with domed roofs that resemble the hogans of the Navajo.

Wood in cordwood lengths is stacked inside these kilns to the very roof. Any type of hardwood is used, but no pine. Pine burns away too fast, leaves very little usable charcoal. Best woods are hickory, elm, ash, oak and sycamore, all native to southern Illinois. Some dogwood, alder and willow are used for certain types of charcoal, as well.

Charcoal, of course, is carbon. There is good and bad. The good charcoal can be tapped with your finger, emitting a faint metallic ring. (This of course, is before it is crushed into brickettes). The rings of the original wood can often be seen, if the burning has been properly controlled. "Tending the fire" is a skill in itself, the amount of air passing into the kiln must always be under rigid control. The fire must be properly smothered, never allowed to leap into tongues of flame.

These are white ash butts, rejected by a
whiskey barrel making plant . . . but they make
fine charcoal.

Pungent white smoke arises from this charcoal plant, where two kilns are burning, while two more are being emptied.

At the Murphysboro Charcoal Company, where these photos were taken, an attendant pointed to a smoking kiln, stating it had been burning for ten days. One more day was needed, then it would be opened to slowly cool.

The average-sized kiln, tightly packed with cordwood and sealed, burns about eleven days. Fire is started at the top, not bottom, works slowly downward. The kiln emits clouds of pungent white smoke during the burning process. If the wind rises, the kilns must be closely watched; if too much air whips up the smoldering fire, often an explosion results.

Southern Illinois farmers and loggers haul wood to these charcoal kilns, sell it at the going price. It's extra income, especially in slack seasons. Once the charcoal is burned it is either bagged for the barbeque trade, or sold in bulk to the steel and affiliated markets.

There is very little statistical information relative to the invention and early development of charcoal. But men learned to make it long before the wheel was dreamed of. For uncounted centuries, charcoal was indispensable to the advance of civilization.

In the dim past, charcoal was the only fuel capable of producing enough heat to soften metal to the point where it could be fashioned into implements and weapons. In time, charcoal, in combination with sulphur and saltpeter, gave us gunpowder.

A vast array of new uses for charcoal have been found. Where once the rural southern Illinois family filtered its drinking water through a barrel filled with charcoal, now the chemical, drug, cosmetics and sugar refining industries use it by the carload for this property alone. In chewing gum, its presence helps to sweeten breath.

Currently, charcoal is a multi-million dollar industry, and the several operations in southern Illinois are doing their part to see that the black stuff is here to stay.

Tobacco and Castor Beans

It seems incongruous today, driving through southern Illinois, that once tobacco and castor beans flourished here, two important industries that did their part to update the economy. But such was the case. There is no visible marker today, pinpointing the castor bean area (Sparta and Chester), but a state-erected plaque reminds the tourist of the tobacco industry that once was part of extreme southern Illinois.

Strange as it might seem today, an article in **The Prairie Farmer** in 1840 cited Randolph County as "The Castor Oil Center of the Nation," with Sparta and Chester both operating oil presses and rivaling for supremacy.

However, the first commercial production did not start in Randolph County but at Edwardsville in Madison County in 1825 when a farmer named Don Adams, experimenting with castor beans as a crop, set up his own presses and produced more than 500 gallons of castor oil that had a commercial value of $2.50 per gallon. Thus encouraged, Adams increased his castor bean acreage and by 1830 was pressing 10,000 gallons of oil yearly.

This gave incentive to a Randolph County man, Richard B. Servant of Chester, who instituted the production of castor oil within his county by furnishing farmers with castor bean seed and advocating that they plant it commercially. Many farmers liked the idea and devoted more and more acreage to castor beans as time passed. Servant set up horse-drawn presses to extract the oil, which in the ensuing years made him a very wealthy man.

Soon after Servant instituted the growing

of castor beans at Chester, a man by the name of James McClurken induced farmers in the Sparta area to get in on this "money crop," and soon the two towns were rivals in the production of castor oil.

Farmers in both the Chester and Sparta region found castor beans a good crop that produced about 20 bushels per acre, with a commerical value of $1.50 or more per bushel.

The production of oil also instituted a new business -- production of tight barrels to hold it, resulting in several small cooper shops in the area.

After 1850, the castor oil crop started to wane, due to the discovery of petroleum and the development of mineral oils. Today, the only castor beans seen in southern Illinois might be a lone plant grown in the garden of some farm.

Many of the early settlers in southern Illinois came from the Appalachians, including Maryland, the Carolinas, Virginia, Tennessee and Kentucky. They were familiar with tobacco culture, and it was only natural they devoted small acreage to the plant in southern Illinois. By 1840, the southern Illinois crop was more than half a million pounds. A decade later it had risen to seven million pounds, advancing to a major crop.

The growing of the crop was an all-year venture. Land had to be carefully prepared, harrowed and raked until the soil had the consistency of sand. Transplanting was a job for spring; the summer was spent in cultivating, topping, worming, and suckering. Then came the curing process, much of it in old-time tobacco barns. Lastly, the crop was loaded on wagons and taken to either Galatia or Raleigh, in Saline County. Here the tobacco was stemmed, bundled into hogsheads, ready for shipment from Shawneetown, where Ohio river boats carried it to market.

Then, like castor oil, tobacco growing started its decline well before the turn of the century, to a complete die-out.

Long Sweetinin'

If you hunt long enough, you'll find it on the shelves of the swankiest supermarkets, dressed up in fancy labels that call it Country Sorghum. Some of it, no doubt, was cooked in Southern Illinois.

Off the highways, in some of the secluded coves of the Shawnee hills, it is still known as 'Long Sweetenin'.'

The name has clung, a folklore of the hills. The name is symbolic of its goodness when poured thick on fluffy biscuits, hot and flaky; on golden, egg-flecked cornbread, on sizzling johnnycakes or bread fresh from the oven. Today it is catalogued as an organic health food, but back at the turn of the century it was simply a staple, a product of the soil.

Called by its proper name, cane sorghum, it has long been a tradition, like pork sausage and sauerkraut. It's always on the shelves of the cluttered rural store. And you'll find it as well stored in kegs in cool, damp cellars of farm homes.

Once cane sorghum was a common staple, and sorghum mills were as numerous as one-room rural schools. But not any more. Less than a dozen still remain in southern Illinois. Each season sees the number lessen. There are a combination of reasons, one of which is very little acreage given to sugar cane.

It took a bit of skill to produce good cane sorghum. Many of the mills were family operations, handed down from one generation to another. But like the Navajo silversmith, the sorghum maker is getting to be a rare breed.

In the old days, cane was crushed by

The Shaw Sorghum Mill, at the junction of
Route 4 and 150, north of Chester, is one of the
few operations still intact in southern Illinois.

horsepower, the animal walking 'round and 'round pulling an overhead beam that in turn operated a roller press. The cane juice was "cooked down" in shallow pans, an evaporation process. When the thickening syrup had the sheen of gold, and ran off the testing spoon in long spiderwebs, it was ready for the jug.

There were other uses for sorghum besides a spread. It was often used in candy making, and was mixed with freshly popped corn to make popcorn balls. It was also used as a medicine. With the addition of a bit of ginger, black pepper and vinegar, it was turned into cough syrup. Like the goose grease that was also used as a remedy for chest colds, whether or not the sorghum helped in stopping coughs is a matter of argument. But one thing is certain: anyone who ever swallowed the mixture learned immediately how pungent it was.

Too bad that the sorghum mill is being erased from the picture. Today, the "butter on our bread" receives very little thought. In pioneer times, however, the procurement of food always presented a problem. Lucky indeed was the family with a cellar well stocked with sorghum, fruit spreads such as apple and peach butter, jams and jellies, all home made. Wild dewberries, blackberries, even persimmons, were preserved for the coming winter. Buying all of these sundries from store shelves was unheard of. If the pioneer family was fortunate enough to own a brindle cow or two, they had home-churned butter. There was also the wild honey often secured by cutting down a good bee tree.

The innovation of sugar cane and the resultant home-cooked sorghum was a blessing. Too bad that the stress of economics is slowly taking the sorghum mill out of the rural picture.

The River Ferryboats

The river ferryboat is one phase of Americana which, according to the statisticians, is slowly vanishing. But not in southern Illinois!

Remember that three rivers, the Mississippi, the Ohio and the Wabash, serve as borderline streams in southern Illinois. There are many spots on these streams where vehicular traffic must cross, yet this same traffic-load is not sufficiently heavy to justify the multi-millions needed to build a modern bridge. Hence the ferry.

Very dedicated men, these ferry operators! Most of them serve long-hour days, winter and summer, at very modest pay. It is a monotonous job, yet there are few complaints, for the river has its own fascination, and some of these men have "catfish milk" in their blood as well.

Starting on the east side of the state, ferries give motorists crossings over the Wabash near Darwin, at St. Francisville, Mount Carmel and Grayville.

Further south, a ferry spans the Ohio at famed Cave-in-Rock, rated busiest in the state. The two barges of this Ohio river ferry can take as many as 27 cars at a time. Carrying as much as four times more traffic than its nearest river competitor, when the river is at flood stage, stopping the traffic, towns in the area literally die economically.

On the west side of southern Illinois, ferries cross the Mississippi at Grand Tower and at Kellogg, across from Ste. Genevieve, Mo. Once a huge railroad ferry shunted freight cars of the Missouri-Illinois Railroad across the river here, but it no longer operates.

Are ferries safe? In most instances they are. The operators are subject to

Wabash Ferries are all similar small boats, for it is a small river. This one crosses the stream at Mt. Carmel.

rigid state inspection, and operation is precise and careful. However, accidents do happen. Not so long ago, the driver of a car came down the ramp of a ferry operating on the Mississippi, apparently had no brakes, and plunged through the guard rails, to his death in the river.

The romance of southern Illinois ferry boats might be typified by a personal experience of one of these operators. Since 1941, a veteran riverman named Ike Caldwell has been operating a ferry over the Wabash at St. Francisville. What made this particular ferry unique was the fact that instead of a conventional engine, Ike had rigged up an old tractor in his ferry engine-house, which powered the boat for no less than 26 years. In that time, the old tractor ran up the astounding "mileage" of 162,000 hours of service.

Then in 1966 the ferry with the tractor engine breathed its last. Ike Caldwell asked a Coast Guard patrolman to keep his eyes open for a good, steel-hulled boat to replace his worn-out ferry.

Months later the Coast Guardsman called him long distance saying he had spotted an exceptionally good boat. But there was a fly in the ointment, so to speak. The boat was far up the Illinois River.

"Why didn't you locate one in Africa?" Ike challenged. "This sounds like the boat I need, but how do I get it home?"

"Just keep it afloat," he was assured, and the guardsman started to explain how this might become an actuality.

In the meantime, Ike was doing a bit of calculating. "Why, that's 800 miles of river!" he said at last.

But thinking it over, he decided that the challenge was something to lick. He had a pilot's license, so there would be no trouble there. He recruited a young friend, asked him if he wanted to take a boat ride.

Starting on the Illinois river, the two men ran the ferry downstream, careful to keep out of the way of the heavy tows, with their long barge trains. Near Pere Marquette State Park they eased their craft from the Illinois to the Mississippi, floating down the big river past St. Louis, all the way to Cairo, Illinois, where they turned upstream into the Ohio. Now the real battle started, fighting the current. Negotiating the locks, they finally reached the mouth of the Wabash, on the last leg home.

But here they ran into even more trouble. At New Harmony, Indiana, the river was so low that they couldn't clear a mill-race. Although the steel-bottomed ferry-boat only drew twelve inches of water empty, they couldn't manipulate the rocks. So they tied up, quite disgusted.

"And then it rained!" Caldwell said, reminiscing. "It really poured, for several hours. The Wabash rose five feet!"

They made the perilous passage over the millrace. At another spot they grounded, and had to have help from a man who provided a tow.

At long last, Caldwell made home port at St. Francisville, after fifteen days and nights of rugged river navigation. The length of the trip was slightly more than 800 miles, with a top speed of ten miles per hour.

So if you cross the Wabash at St. Francisville, take special note of the ferry. This one has been a real gypsy.